Apress Pocket Guides

Apress Pocket Guides present concise summaries of cutting-edge developments and working practices throughout the tech industry. Shorter in length, books in this series aims to deliver quick-to-read guides that are easy to absorb, perfect for the time-poor professional.

This series covers the full spectrum of topics relevant to the modern industry, from security, AI, machine learning, cloud computing, web development, product design, to programming techniques and business topics too.

Typical topics might include:

- A concise guide to a particular topic, method, function or framework

- Professional best practices and industry trends

- A snapshot of a hot or emerging topic

- Industry case studies

- Concise presentations of core concepts suited for students and those interested in entering the tech industry

- Short reference guides outlining 'need-to-know' concepts and practices.

More information about this series at `https://link.springer.com/bookseries/17385`.

Technical Writing for Developers

Utilizing HTML, JavaScript, Markdown, and GitHub for Writing

Jim Hall

Apress®

Technical Writing for Developers: Utilizing HTML, JavaScript, Markdown, and GitHub for Writing

Jim Hall
St Paul, MN, USA

ISBN-13 (pbk): 979-8-8688-2110-3 ISBN-13 (electronic): 979-8-8688-2111-0
https://doi.org/10.1007/979-8-8688-2111-0

Copyright © 2025 by Jim Hall

This work is subject to copyright. All rights are reserved by the Publisher, whether the whole or part of the material is concerned, specifically the rights of translation, reprinting, reuse of illustrations, recitation, broadcasting, reproduction on microfilms or in any other physical way, and transmission or information storage and retrieval, electronic adaptation, computer software, or by similar or dissimilar methodology now known or hereafter developed.

Trademarked names, logos, and images may appear in this book. Rather than use a trademark symbol with every occurrence of a trademarked name, logo, or image we use the names, logos, and images only in an editorial fashion and to the benefit of the trademark owner, with no intention of infringement of the trademark.

The use in this publication of trade names, trademarks, service marks, and similar terms, even if they are not identified as such, is not to be taken as an expression of opinion as to whether or not they are subject to proprietary rights.

While the advice and information in this book are believed to be true and accurate at the date of publication, neither the authors nor the editors nor the publisher can accept any legal responsibility for any errors or omissions that may be made. The publisher makes no warranty, express or implied, with respect to the material contained herein.

    Managing Director, Apress Media LLC: Welmoed Spahr
    Acquisitions Editor: James Robinson-Prior
    Coordinating Editor: Gryffin Winkler

Cover designed by eStudioCalamar

Distributed to the book trade worldwide by Springer Science+Business Media New York, 1 New York Plaza, New York, NY 10004. Phone 1-800-SPRINGER, fax (201) 348-4505, e-mail orders-ny@springer-sbm.com, or visit www.springeronline.com. Apress Media, LLC is a Delaware LLC and the sole member (owner) is Springer Science + Business Media Finance Inc (SSBM Finance Inc). SSBM Finance Inc is a Delaware corporation.

For information on translations, please e-mail booktranslations@springernature.com; for reprint, paperback, or audio rights, please e-mail bookpermissions@springernature.com.

Apress titles may be purchased in bulk for academic, corporate, or promotional use. eBook versions and licenses are also available for most titles. For more information, reference our Print and eBook Bulk Sales web page at http://www.apress.com/bulk-sales.

Any source code or other supplementary material referenced by the author in this book is available to readers on GitHub (https://github.com/Apress). For more detailed information, please visit https://www.apress.com/gp/services/source-code.

If disposing of this product, please recycle the paper

With love to Sara, my wife.

Table of Contents

About the Author xi

About the Technical Reviewer xiii

Acknowledgments xv

An Introduction to Technical Writing for Developers xvii

Chapter 1: The Basics of HTML 1
   Collecting Words and Filling Paragraphs 1
   HTML Elements Are Either Block or Inline 2
   Other HTML Elements 4
   Finishing HTML Documents 5
   HTML Quick Reference Guide 7
      Block elements 8
      Inline elements 8

Chapter 2: Three Tips to Create Accessible HTML Documents 9
   Alternative Text for Images 10
   Semantic Markup 11
   Captions in Figures 14

Chapter 3: Write HTML Documents with Style 17
   Start with an HTML Document 17
   Let Styles Do the Work for You 19
   Single-Use Stylesheets 22

TABLE OF CONTENTS

Chapter 4: Writing Technical Documents in HTML..................25
A Sample Program 25
Documenting Input and Output 27
Heading and Paragraphs..28
Input and Output 30
Program Output As Blocks 32

Chapter 5: Try It: Writing Your Own Web Pages.....................37
Elements and Structure 37
Change the Look 41
Update the Styles..45

Chapter 6: Write Dynamic Web Documentation with JavaScript........51
Structuring Content with Classes 51
Use Classes for Each Audience 55
Add JavaScript to Control the View...58
Make the JavaScript Flexible for the User 62

Chapter 7: Introduction to Markdown 69
Getting Started in Markdown 69
Basic Formatting...71
Add Structure with Headings 72
Markdown Makes It Easy 76

Chapter 8: Markup with Markdown..77
Ordered and Unordered Lists 77
Block Quotes 80
Hyperlinks 81
Tables...82
Verbatim Text 85

viii

TABLE OF CONTENTS

Chapter 9: GitHub for Technical Writers 93
How Source Control Works 93
Managing Versions in GitHub 99

Chapter 10: Next Steps 109
Use What You've Learned 110
Take It to the Next Level 114

About the Author

Jim Hall has spent the last 30 years at the intersection of open source technology and technical writing, contributing to open source projects since the 1990s, and has been a technical writer since 2010. Jim is the founder of Technically We Write and Coaching Buttons; has been a regular contributor to *Linux Journal,* Opensource.com, *Enable Sysadmin, Enable Architect, Enterprisers Project,* Both.org, and *All Things Open*; and enjoys writing articles about how things work, including programming, Linux, command line, and other open source and web development tools and applications.

About the Technical Reviewer

Seth Kenlon is a Linux and UNIX geek. A user of Slackware for decades, he's a Java and Lua programmer, a documentation writer (with a preference for Asciidoc and Docbook), a member of the Internet Press Guild, and a frequent contributor to open source. In his spare time, he's an avid tabletop gamer and hobbyist game designer.

Acknowledgments

This book would not be possible without the support of many people. Thank you to my friends, colleagues, and everyone else that I have worked with over the years. You've helped me to learn and grow.

Thank you to David for making the connection and to Seth for providing the review.

An Introduction to Technical Writing for Developers

Everyone does technical writing of some kind, no matter what their role is in the organization. This is true especially for developers and systems administrators, who often need to create guides and other documentation for others in their team.

This is a "how-to" book about using markup for technical writing. With this book, you'll get a fast "dive" into how to use markup systems for the most common formatting in technical writing. Look at any poll or "top 5" list published today and you'll find HTML and Markdown at the top of the markup systems that technical users need to know. And that's what we'll focus on in the book.

HTML is Hyper Text Markup Language, and it is what drives the World Wide Web. While most modern websites are constructed using a web content management system like Drupal or WordPress, knowing how to create a website by writing HTML can be a handy skill. You don't need special software to translate or transform an HTML document into a readable form; you only need a web browser.

In Chapter 1, we'll learn the basics of how to write in HTML and to create documents that work everywhere. You can use Chrome, Safari, Firefox, Opera, and Edge—or mobile browsers on Android and iPhone—to view what you write in HTML to immediately see the results. With HTML, you can write a document and immediately see it "in action" on a browser.

We'll build on this knowledge in Chapter 2 as we learn how to create useful and accessible documentation that everyone can use. Semantic markup, alternative text, and captions will allow you to write documentation that everyone can use, including those with diminished or no vision. Websites should be for everyone.

But HTML doesn't have to be plain black-on-white text. In Chapter 3, we'll learn how to use styles to improve the appearance of HTML documents so they look more professional. By defining a few styles in a stylesheet, we can make important information stand out, highlight important information, and generally make web documentation easier to read.

In Chapter 4, we'll expand what we have learned about HTML to cover more technical documentation with HTML, including how to format output, and inline and block code samples.

We'll take this even further in Chapter 5 as we explore how to write your own full web pages and websites by hand in HTML.

For cases where you need to write one document that supports a wide range of experienced or inexperienced users, consider writing dynamic documentation. In Chapter 6, we will learn how to apply some simple JavaScript to let your audience choose what information they need to see.

HTML is a great way to write documentation for the web. You don't have to be a developer to write in HTML; anyone can use a plain text editor to create HTML documents that you can view right in a web browser.

But sometimes, you might want to focus on the content of your message without getting distracted by what it will look like. That's why the last few chapters of this book transition to writing with Markdown, a minimal markup system.

In Chapter 7, we'll see that Markdown borrows much of its formatting from how people would normally write documentation in plain text: paragraphs are just lines of text separated by blank lines. Headings and subheadings use an "underline" effect with dashes, and bold and italic text use "underscore" and asterisks like you are probably already used to writing in plain text emails.

In Chapter 8, we'll take a deep dive into other formatting that you can do with Markdown, such as lists, block quotes, links, code, and tables. Markdown makes it easy to write technical documentation without really thinking about the formatting to get there.

Markdown is a popular system that's "baked in" with other source code control systems like GitHub. So in Chapter 9, we will learn about how technical writers can leverage GitHub to collaborate with technical teams. If you haven't used source code control systems before, we will start with an overview of how source control works and then demonstrate how to use GitHub to manage files.

HTML and Markdown are excellent starting points for writing with markup, but they aren't the only markup systems you can use. In the conclusion of the book in Chapter 10, we'll see that by learning how to write with HTML and Markdown, you've also opened the door to learning other markup systems.

For example, HTML is a great "launching point" for learning other tag-based markup like XML. Lots of other modern markup systems are based on XML, so this introduction to HTML is also a way to get started with XML-based markup like DITA and Docbook.

And by learning Markdown, you've also learned the same basic techniques that are used in other minimal markup systems. Another popular system is AsciiDoc, which isn't too different from Markdown. If you needed to transition to AsciiDoc, you can leverage what you learned about writing in Markdown to quickly become productive in AsciiDoc or other minimal markup systems.

Let's get started!

CHAPTER 1

The Basics of HTML

Hyper Text Markup Language, or HTML, is arguably the most widely used markup system in the world. While other markup systems are out there, including older document preparation markup systems like LaTeX and nroff, and newer XML-based markup systems including Docbook and DITA, HTML remains the most used markup system because it is the language that allows us to write for the web.

First implemented in web browsers like Mosaic and then Netscape Navigator in 1994, HTML has evolved and added new features over time, but the basics remain the same: HTML is plain text and uses simple tags called elements to control formatting. This starting point makes it easy to get started with writing in HTML.

Collecting Words and Filling Paragraphs

Let's start with a basic understanding of HTML and how client applications like web browsers display HTML documents. At its most basic level, HTML collects words and fills paragraphs. Without other markup, a web browser will collect words in a document and use them to fill a block paragraph. For example, if we create a plain text file called `sample.html` and write a sample paragraph of text, a web browser would display or render the contents like a block paragraph:

```
Every web page in every web site is delivered to a
```

```
user's web browser in HTML format.
That's a lot of web pages.
```

You can save this file to your computer or on a web server and access it from your web browser like you would any website. How you access the file doesn't really matter; it can be remote on a web server or local on your own computer. But you should always name an HTML document with the .html file extension, so web browsers will recognize it as HTML content.

In this case, I've written the content on separate lines. I've also added an extra blank line to demonstrate that HTML doesn't really care about extra white space in a file. Adding extra lines or spaces helps humans to read the source code, but the web browser instead examines the content using tags to control formatting. Without these tags, the browser collects the words and fills a paragraph as though the file were written on one line. Viewed in a web browser, this file looks like this:

> Every web page in every web site is delivered to a user's web browser in HTML format. That's a lot of web pages.

Figure 1-1. *The sample.html file, as viewed in a web browser*

HTML Elements Are Either Block or Inline

To format an HTML document, you need to add HTML elements in the form of tags. Using elements and tags requires knowing only a few rules:

- HTML elements are written as tags
- Write a tag as a control word between angle brackets, such as `<html>`
- Most tags come in pairs: a start tag and an end tag

HTML elements are either block or inline. Most HTML tags are some kind of a block element or inline element, so it helps to start with just these two to understand how they work.

You can think of a block element as always filling a rectangle, and an inline element as following just the text. The most basic example of a block element is the `<div>` tag to define a division on a web page. A division doesn't do any formatting on its own, except that any text between the opening `<div>` and closing `</div>` tags will be displayed as a block element. The basic inline element is the `<span>` tag. A span doesn't add any formatting; it only collects inline text.

Let's add some `<div>` and `<span>` tags to the sample document to see what block and inline elements look like:

```
<div>Every web page in every web site is delivered to a
user's web browser in HTML format.
<span>That's a lot of web pages.</span>
</div>
```

I've added a `<div>` block element around the entire paragraph, and a `<span>` inline element around just one sentence. For each opening HTML tag, I also included the closing tag: `</span>` and `</div>`. Almost all elements are written like this, with opening and closing tags. These tags need to be opened and closed in the same order. If you start a `<span>` within a `<div>`, you need to end the span with `</span>` before you end the division with `</div>`.

The web browser interprets these tags to display the HTML content in a certain way, but because the `<div>` and `<span>` elements don't provide any special formatting, the web browser will display the text in the same way as though no tags were applied.

> Every web page in every web site is delivered to a user's web browser in HTML format. That's a lot of web pages.

Figure 1-2. *The updated sample.html file looks the same*

We can include direct styling in these tags by adding a `style` attribute. An attribute is something that modifies an element, almost like an argument to a command-line program. In this case, we can add a `style` attribute to put a gray border around the division, and display the span in bold text:

```
<div style="border:1px solid gray">Every web page in every web
site is delivered to a user's web browser in HTML format.
<span style="font-weight:bold">That's a lot of web
pages.</span>
</div>
```

With these edits, the entire text is surrounded by a gray border. Because this is a division with the `<div>` element, this fills a rectangle. The second sentence is inside a `<span>` element, which follows the text:

> Every web page in every web site is delivered to a user's web browser in HTML format. **That's a lot of web pages.**

Figure 1-3. The updated sample.html file, as viewed in a web browser

Other HTML Elements

HTML defines over a hundred elements that you can use to format documents, and they are either block-like `<div>` or inline-like `<span>`. The key difference is that `<div>` and `<span>` do not provide any default formatting, but most other elements do.

One common element is `<p>` to define a paragraph. This is a block element, similar to `<div>`, but has some extra space above and below the paragraph.

Headings use <h1> through <h6>, and use different font sizes, in a bold weight, with extra space above and below the headings.

The <strong> element is an inline element that displays text in a bold weight.

Similarly, <em> is an inline element that formats text in italic style.

For example, we could use the <p> paragraph element to format the paragraph instead of using a division, and use the <strong> inline element to provide strong emphasis instead of using a span. At the same time, we can write the title of the document using <h1>, like this:

```
<h1>About HTML</h1>

<p>Every web page in every web site is delivered to a
user's web browser in HTML format.

<strong>That's a lot of web pages.</strong>
</p>
```

Without the extra `style` attribute, the document will look quite plain, but we only used the styles to highlight the block and inline elements. There are better ways to apply custom styles to documents; we will learn about that in Chapter 3.

About HTML

Every web page in every web site is delivered to a user's web browser in HTML format. **That's a lot of web pages.**

Figure 1-4. *The updated sample.html file, with a heading for the title*

Finishing HTML Documents

Some elements are required to make a document technically valid. While the sample HTML document from above will display correctly in a web browser, it is not a technically valid HTML document. The HTML standard also requires that web content is "wrapped" in two other block elements: `<html>` to define an HTML document, and `<body>` to indicate the body text. To ensure the document will be interpreted correctly, you must also declare its document type with the DOCTYPE tag at the top of the document.

```
<!DOCTYPE html>
<html>
  <body>
  ..
  </body>
</html>
```

Every document also needs to define certain metadata, using a `<head>` document header before the body text. At a minimum, the header must declare the document's title with the `<title>` element. With these elements, we can define a minimally valid HTML document:

```
<!DOCTYPE html>
<html>
  <head>
    <title>..</title>
  </head>
  <body>
  ..
  </body>
</html>
```

Let's add the code that we wrote above. To insert this content as the text body, place it inside the `<body>` element. We should also update the title of the document; while this doesn't need to be the same title text that is used in the `<h1>` element, it is usually a good idea to make them the same:

```html
<!DOCTYPE html>
<html>
  <head>
    <title>About HTML</title>
  </head>
  <body>
    <h1>About HTML</h1>

    <p>Every web page in every web site is delivered to a
    user's web browser in HTML format.

    <strong>That's a lot of web pages.</strong>
    </p>
  </body>
</html>
```

When viewed in a web browser, the document looks the same as before. But this version is now technically valid because it contains the elements that are required for any HTML document:

About HTML

Every web page in every web site is delivered to a user's web browser in HTML format. **That's a lot of web pages.**

Figure 1-5. *The updated sample.html file, as a technically valid HTML document*

HTML Quick Reference Guide

With so many HTML elements to use to format documents, finding the right one may seem like a tough challenge. Use this quick reference guide for these common HTML elements. These aren't all of the elements available to format HTML documents, but these will get you pretty far:

Block elements

Block element	What it does
`<h1>` to `<h6>`	Headings
`<p>`	Paragraphs
`<pre>`	Pre-formatted text (keep line breaks)
`<ol>`	Ordered lists (numbered lists)
`<ul>`	Unordered lists (bullet lists)
`<li>`	List item (for either `<ol>` or `<ul>`)
`<blockquote>`	Block quotes

Inline elements

Table Head	Table Head
`<em>`	Emphasis (italic text)
`<strong>`	Strong emphasis (bold text)
`<cite>`	Citations, such as book titles
`<code>`	Code samples, can also be used inside `<pre>`
`<samp>`	Sample output from a computer program
`<kbd>`	Keyboard input or other user input
`<q>`	Inline quotes (also adds quote marks)

CHAPTER 2

Three Tips to Create Accessible HTML Documents

It's easy to think that everyone will be able to read the documents that we create, especially if we create them digitally using a markup system like HTML. But the reality is that some people will not be able to access content in the same way.

For example, some readers might be blind, so they rely on assistive technology to "read" web pages to them. Other readers might have diminished vision, such as poor eyesight or low contrast vision, so the content will appear fuzzy.

And others might see well but not in color. Some might have complete color loss, and can only see in shades of black and white, while others might not see specific colors, such as protanopia and deuteranopia, which are two common types of red-green color blindness.

Also consider situational accessibility needs. For example, many mobile devices like phones will switch to a black and white mode in the evening, to help users "unplug" and go to sleep. Anyone who views web content on a phone at night will be temporarily unable to see in color, even though they otherwise have color vision.

Of course, your web pages aren't just for your website visitors. Websites can also be scanned by search engines and other systems that can summarize information. By providing content that is accessible to all, you also make your websites easier for search engines to parse, which in turn can give your website a higher "score" for SEO, or Search Engine Optimization.

If you create digital content such as websites, it's critical that you create content that meets people where they are. If our audience cannot read or otherwise access the content we create, then we have failed as communicators. That means you need to be careful to create accessible content.

HTML provides several methods that you can use to support accessibility. Here are several ways to make your content more accessible to your audience.

Alternative Text for Images

HTML documents can use `<img>` tag to include an image, such as a photo or diagram or logo. However, not everyone can see an image, such as those with total vision loss.

When including images in documents, don't forget to include the `alt` attribute to provide alternative text for your readers. This alternative text is required by the HTML standard, and will be used by screen readers and other assistive technologies to provide a description of the image for those who cannot see it.

For example, let's say you wanted to include a screenshot of a progress bar, as part of a discussion for how to install software. You might use this image reference for the screenshot:

```
<img src="screenshots/progress.png"
  alt="a progress bar showing 50 percent complete">
```

Avoid describing the image as "screenshot of" or "photo or" or "image of." Most screen readers will start the description using "image of" or "image," so using "image of" in your alternative text will "read" as "image of image of." Without it, the assistive technology will instead describe the image as "image of a progress bar showing 50 percent complete."

The alternative text must be descriptive of the image. Try to write a brief one-sentence "word picture" that describes what is in the image. For example, using the word "photo" would not provide enough detail to describe an image with meaningful detail:

```
<img src="assets/31422-27693-29466.jpg"
  alt="photo">
```

Semantic Markup

In the early days of the web, authors created web pages using a very simple structure. In those cases, it was typical to divide a page using `<div>` tags, such as a simple page with a header, navigation bar, main body, and footer, like this:

```
<html>
  <head>
    <title>..</title>
  </head>
  <body>
    <div class="hdr">
      <img src="logo.svg" alt="a black filled circle">
      Company Name
    </div>

    <div class="navbar">
      <a href="/">Home</a>
```

```
    <a href="/about.html">About us</a>
  </div>

  <div class="bdy">
    ..
  </div>

  <div class="ftr">
    <p>Copyright 2002</p>
  </div>
 </body>
</html>
```

This creates a web page that might look great in a web browser, but provides no information hierarchy to describe the web page's organization:

● Company Name
Home About us
..

Copyright 2002

Figure 2-1. *The web page, as viewed in a web browser*

However, `<div>` carries no special meaning or formatting by itself. The `class` attribute is useful only to web browsers, to style the content using a style sheet. As a result, anyone who uses a screen reader to browse the web will have no option but to have the entire page read to them.

In 2008, HTML version 5 introduced semantic markup, which provides meaning to the tags that make up a web page. Most web pages have a header, navigation, main body, and footer, so HTML 5 defined new tags to provide that structure, including `<header>`, `<nav>`, `<main>`, and `<footer>`.

HTML 5 also included other meaningful elements such as `<section>` for larger divisions of a page and `<article>` for content that might be an article or other information item.

These semantic tags can be used anywhere in an HTML document. For example, the <body> might have a header, main body, and footer, but <article> content might have the same elements, as well. Also, the <header> in a web page might contain navigation links with <nav>, or the <body> might contain "bread crumb" navigation links, also with <nav>.

The semantic markup also helps users to navigate a website using screen readers or other assistive technology. Depending on the software, the screen reader might announce "header" when it encounters a page header, then the user can press a key to skip ahead to the next major section, such as the main body.

Structuring an HTML document using semantics provides a more logical organization to the web page. For example, we might rewrite the sample web page from above to use HTML 5 semantic tags, like this:

```
<!DOCTYPE html>
<html>
  <head>
    <title>..</title>
  </head>

  <body>
    <header>
      <img src="logo.svg" alt="a black filled circle">
      Company Name
    </header>

    <nav>
      <a href="/">Home</a>
      <a href="/about.html">About us</a>
    </nav>

    <main>
      ..
    </main>
```

CHAPTER 2   THREE TIPS TO CREATE ACCESSIBLE HTML DOCUMENTS

```
    <footer>
      <p>Copyright 2002</p>
    </footer>
  </body>
</html>
```

This updated HTML document looks the same in a web browser, but also has the extra information in the semantic elements to make the page accessible to users with screen readers:

Figure 2-2. *The updated web page looks the same in a web browser*

Captions in Figures

HTML version 5 didn't add semantic markup simply to provide structure to HTML documents. Many of the HTML semantic elements also enhance accessibility. One such feature is the <figure> block element, which acts as a container for images, charts, graphs, and other kinds of data displays.

Figure can include captions using the optional <figcaption> element, and I recommend using it whenever you can. A figure caption should describe the image in a complementary way to the image's alternative text. Don't repeat the alternative text as the figure caption; instead, use the alternative text to provide the image description and the caption to provide the context for the image.

Let's say you're writing an HTML document as the "Readme" for a software program, and you want to include a screenshot of what the program looks like when it is running. You might include this image in a document using <figure> to contain the image, and <figcaption> to provide a caption:

```
<figure>
  <img src="screenshot.png"
    alt="a progress bar at the 25% mark">
  <figcaption>Saving your work takes only a few seconds</figcaption>
</figure>
```

Note that the alternative text describes the image itself, which helps readers who rely on a screen reader or other assistive technology. Meanwhile, the figure caption provides additional contextual information about the image. The caption must be either the first or last element inside the figure.

Saving your work takes only a few seconds

CHAPTER 3

Write HTML Documents with Style

HTML makes it easy to publish content in a way that your audience can read via their web browser. HTML documentation doesn't have to be served from a website; it can be shared in a folder in a GitHub repository, or provided in some other way. As long as the content is written in HTML, any browser will be able to display it

You can write documentation in plain HTML, and that will get the job done. But you can make details stand out if you apply a few simple styles.

Start with an HTML Document

Let's see how documentation can be made easier to read by adding a few styles. To demonstrate, we'll need to have an HTML document, something typical of most technical documents written in HTML, like a short "how-to" document about writing Linux shell scripts in Bash.

Every HTML document starts as this minimally valid HTML document:

```
<!DOCTYPE html>
<html>
  <head>
    <title>..</title>
  </head>
```

```
  <body>
  ..
  </body>
</html>
```

We can fill in the blanks by writing a short document about scripting in Bash. As a technical document, this might include emphasis with `<em>`, strong emphasis with `<strong>`, and inline code with `<code>` for things like variable names.

```
<!DOCTYPE html>
<html>
  <head>
    <title>Variables in Bash scripts</title>
  </head>
  <body>
    <h1>Variables in Bash scripts</h1>
    <p><strong>Try to make your variable names
    meaningful.</strong>
    Avoid single-letter variable names like <code>a</code> or
    too-short abbreviations like <code>tmsk</code>.
    While these names may be meaningful to <em>you</em>,
    they will be confusing to <em>someone else</em>.
    Instead, choose variable names that describe the
    value they will store, like <code>count</code> or
    <code>size</code>.</p>
  </body>
</html>
```

When viewed in a web browser, this adequately describes how to write variables in Bash scripts, but it doesn't have much visual flair. More importantly, some users may have difficulty distinguishing the change in font when the page displays sample code, especially for very short text that is only a few letters long.

Variables in Bash scripts

Try to **make your variable names meaningful.** Avoid single-letter variable names like a or too-short abbreviations like tmsk. While these names may be meaningful to *you*, they will be confusing to *someone else*. Instead, choose variable names that describe the value they will store, like count or size.

Figure 3-1. *The sample text, as viewed in a web browser*

Let Styles Do the Work for You

You can apply styles like fonts and colors to this HTML document to make it easier to read. Styles get defined in the document header in the <head> block, with other metadata, and apply to the entire file. You can reference a separate file for the styles by adding a <link> tag, which creates a relationship to a "stylesheet," like this:

```
<!DOCTYPE html>
<html>
  <head>
    <title>..</title>
    <link rel="stylesheet" href="styles.css">
  </head>
  <body>
  ..
  </body>
</html>
```

CHAPTER 3   WRITE HTML DOCUMENTS WITH STYLE

As a metadata element, the `<link>` tag is one of the few HTML tags that does not have a closing tag; there is no `</link>` tag to close the `<link>` tag.

```
<!DOCTYPE html>
<html>
  <head>
    <title>Variables in Bash scripts</title>
    <link rel="stylesheet" href="styles.css">
  </head>
  <body>
    <h1>Variables in Bash scripts</h1>
    <p><strong>Try to make your variable names
    meaningful.</strong>
    Avoid single-letter variable names like <code>a</code> or
    too-short abbreviations like <code>tmsk</code>.
    While these names may be meaningful to <em>you</em>,
    they will be confusing to <em>someone else</em>.
    Instead, choose variable names that describe the value they
    will store, like <code>count</code> or <code>size</code>.</p>
  </body>
</html>
```

Stylesheets do not look like HTML. Instead, the stylesheet format was inspired by the C programming language. To see what I mean, let's examine a trivial C program that prints the text "Hello world" and then immediately exits. The program is called `main` and the statements that make up the program go inside `{` and `}` curly braces, and end with `;` semicolon.

```
#include <stdio.h>

int main() {
  puts("Hello world");
  return 0;
}
```

Styles in a stylesheet file look like that. To apply styles to an HTML element, start by naming the element, then enter the style definitions inside { and } curly braces, ending each definition with ; semicolon. With stylesheets, write each definition as `name:value` pairs, with an optional space after the colon.

Like the C programming language, you could also write the entire style definition on one line and rely on the semicolon to terminate a statement. However, your style definitions will be more readable if you put each statement on its own line.

Since we're just learning about stylesheets, let's demonstrate with a basic kind of style: the background color. To help the inline code samples stand out from the rest of the text, we can define a new style for the `<code>` tag like this:

```
code {
  background-color: lightgray;
}
```

Save this three-line file as `styles.css` in the same directory as your sample HTML document. Then the `<link rel="stylesheet" href="styles.css">` link relationship in the HTML document's `<head>` section will reference this stylesheet file. With everything in the right place, we can see the result by viewing the HTML file in a web browser:

Variables in Bash scripts

Try to make your variable names meaningful. Avoid single-letter variable names like `a` or too-short abbreviations like `tmsk`. While these names may be meaningful to *you*, they will be confusing to *someone else*. Instead, choose variable names that describe the value they will store, like `count` or `size`.

Figure 3-2. *The sample text, as viewed in a web browser*

Saving your styles in a stylesheet is an excellent choice if you need to refer back to the same styles all the time. For example, if you need to write several documents and want them all to have the same look and feel, you might link all of your HTML documents to the same stylesheet file.

CHAPTER 3   WRITE HTML DOCUMENTS WITH STYLE

Single-Use Stylesheets

Sometimes, you only need to write a stylesheet that will apply to one file. While you can link to a separate stylesheet file, it can be very handy to define a single-use stylesheet for "one-off" documentation. Use `<style>` to embed a stylesheet within an HTML document. Like the `<link>` tag, this goes inside the `<head>` section of the HTML document with the other metadata:

```
<!DOCTYPE html>
<html>
  <head>
    <title>..</title>
    <style>..</style>
  </head>
  <body>
  ..
  </body>
</html>
```

The syntax of the stylesheet is the same as before: apply your own styles to an element by naming the element, and enter the styles between `{` and `}` curly braces. Each style definition is a `name:value` pair, and ends with a `;` (semicolon). For example, we might have written the HTML example using an embedded stylesheet using `<style>` for the stylesheet.

```
<!DOCTYPE html>
<html>
  <head>
    <title>Variables in Bash scripts</title>
    <style>
```

```
    code {
      background-color: lightgray;
    }
  </style>
</head>
<body>
  <h1>Variables in Bash scripts</h1>
  <p><strong>Try to make your variable names
  meaningful.</strong>
  Avoid single-letter variable names like <code>a</code> or
  too-short abbreviations like <code>tmsk</code>.
  While these names may be meaningful to <em>you</em>,
  they will be confusing to <em>someone else</em>.
  Instead, choose variable names that describe the
  value they will store, like <code>count</code> or
  <code>size</code>.</p>
</body>
</html>
```

If we save this new file, we can see the result by viewing the HTML file in a web browser:

Variables in Bash scripts

Try to make your variable names meaningful. Avoid single-letter variable names like `a` or too-short abbreviations like `tmsk`. While these names may be meaningful to *you*, they will be confusing to *someone else*. Instead, choose variable names that describe the value they will store, like `count` or `size`.

Figure 3-3. *The sample text, as viewed in a web browser*

Using a single-use stylesheet is not a bad choice if you need to write one HTML document, where a separate stylesheet file is just extra file management that you don't need for your project.

CHAPTER 4

Writing Technical Documents in HTML

Good documentation is important for any technical project. This documentation might be building notes that describe how to compile the system, test plans with information about what input should produce what output, or "readme" files that contain general notes about the program.

For many projects, plain text format is the standard because every system can display plain text. But plain text is very limiting; it lacks formatting that lets certain kinds of text stand out, like italic text, bold text, inline code, and section headings. To add these elements, we can leverage HTML. By leveraging the available HTML tags, you can make your documentation more readable to anyone with a web browser.

A Sample Program

Let's exercise some HTML knowledge by writing a sample "readme" file using HTML. As we saw in earlier chapters, HTML has a standard boilerplate, which starts as a minimally valid HTML document. While HTML doesn't require indenting each new code block, I'll add it anyway so you can see the different "levels," such as that the <body> block is "inside" the <html> block:

CHAPTER 4   WRITING TECHNICAL DOCUMENTS IN HTML

```
<!DOCTYPE html>
<html>
  <head>
    <title>..</title>
  </head>
  <body>
    ..
  </body>
</html>
```

For this example, let's describe a simple "Guess the Number" game. In this game, the computer picks a random value and the user must guess that secret number. The program prints "Too low" or "Too high" to help the user with each guess, and prints "That's right!" when the guess is correct.

This game is a popular way to explore computing, because it has a fairly simple structure that makes it easy to follow. You can write your own "Guess the Number" in any programming language, including the Bash shell:

```
#!/bin/bash
echo 'Guess a random number from 1 to 100'
secret=$(( RANDOM % 100 + 1 ))
guess=0

until [ $secret -eq "$guess" ] ; do
  echo -n 'Your guess? '
  read guess
  [ "$guess" -lt $secret ] && echo 'Too low'
  [ "$guess" -gt $secret ] && echo 'Too high'
done

echo "That's right!"
```

But no matter how trivial the program might be, we still need to write good documentation to help new users learn how to play the game.

Documenting Input and Output

Let's start by writing a plain text version of a "readme" file that describes how to play the game:

```
Guess the Number

How to play:

The game starts by describing the basic rules: you need
to guess a secret number.

  Guess a random number from 1 to 100

Enter your guess for the secret number and the program
will provide a hint:

  * "Too low" if your guess is too low
  * "Too high" if your guess is too high

Let's say the secret number is 33. You might enter 50 as
your first guess. The program will print this:

  Too high

For your next guess, you could try the number 25, which
is halfway between 1 and 50. The program then displays:

  Too low

After several more guesses, you eventually enter 33, and
the program prints:

  That's right!
```

    This sample text has typical elements for a technical document, including a title, section heading, a list, and multiple paragraphs. And because the "readme" describes an interactive program, it also provides several examples of user input and sample output.

CHAPTER 4 WRITING TECHNICAL DOCUMENTS IN HTML

Heading and Paragraphs

The first step to format this "readme" as an HTML document is to enter the text between the <body> and </body> tags. Let's start with <h1> for the title, <h2> for the section heading, <ul> and <li> for the list, and <p> for each paragraph. To keep things simple in this step, we can format the program output as a normal paragraph:

```
<!DOCTYPE html>
<html>
  <head>
    <title>Guess the Number</title>
  </head>
  <body>
<h1>Guess the Number</h1>

<h2>How to play:</h2>

<p>The game starts by describing the basic rules: you need to guess a secret number.</p>

<p>Guess a random number from 1 to 100</p>

<p>Enter your guess for the secret number and the program will provide a hint:</p>

<ul>
  <li>"Too low" if your guess is too low</li>
  <li>"Too high" if your guess is too high</li>
</ul>

<p>Let's say the secret number is 33. You might enter 50 as your first guess. The program will print this:</p>

<p>Too high</p>
```

CHAPTER 4   WRITING TECHNICAL DOCUMENTS IN HTML

```
<p>For your next guess, you could try the number 25, which
is halfway between 1 and 50. The program then displays:</p>

<p>Too low</p>

<p>After several more guesses, you eventually enter 33, and
the program prints:</p>

<p>That's right!</p>
  </body>
</html>
```

This is a good first approximation of a "readme" in HTML, but it doesn't provide any extra formatting to indicate what the user might enter into the system, and what the program might print to the screen. Because everything is just paragraphs, there's nothing to suggest what is user input or program output:

Guess the Number

How to play:

The game starts by describing the basic rules: you need to guess a secret number.

Guess a random number from 1 to 100

Enter your guess for the secret number and the program will provide a hint:

- "Too low" if your guess is too low
- "Too high" if your guess is too high

Let's say the secret number is 33. You might enter 50 as your first guess. The program will print this:

Too high

For your next guess, you could try the number 25, which is halfway between 1 and 50. The program then displays:

Too low

After several more guesses, you eventually enter 33, and the program prints:

That's right!

Input and Output

One way to indicate input and output is to use bold and italic text, but this is a very simple approximation. It might be tempting to use `<code>` to represent these, but HTML provides several tags dedicated for input and output:

- `<kbd>` represents text that a user might enter on a keyboard
- `<samp>` encloses sample output from a program

Both of these tags are inline elements that should be enclosed by a parent block element, such as `<p>` for paragraph text or `<pre>` for a block of preformatted text. Let's apply these tags to the "readme" document:

```
<!DOCTYPE html>
<html>
  <head>
    <title>Guess the Number</title>
  </head>
  <body>
<h1>Guess the Number</h1>

<h2>How to play:</h2>

<p>The game starts by describing the basic rules: you need
to guess a secret number.</p>

<pre><samp>Guess a random number from 1 to 100</samp></pre>

<p>Enter your guess for the secret number and the program
will provide a hint:</p>

<ul>
  <li><samp>Too low</samp> if your guess is too low</li>
```

```
  <li><samp>Too high</samp> if your guess is too high</li>
</ul>
```

```
<p>Let's say the secret number is 33. You might enter <kbd>50
</kbd> as your first guess. The program will print this:</p>
```

```
<pre><samp>Too high</samp></pre>
```

```
<p>For your next guess, you could try the number <kbd>25</kbd>,
which is halfway between 1 and 50. The program then displays:</p>
```

```
<pre><samp>Too low</samp></pre>
```

```
<p>After several more guesses, you eventually enter <kbd>33</
kbd>, and the program prints:</p>
```

```
<pre><samp>That's right!</samp></pre>
  </body>
</html>
```

By formatting user input and program output with these extra tags, the document is now much easier to read. The HTML standard does not specify how the <kbd> and <samp> tags should appear in a document, but most web browsers will display them using a typewriter-like font.

CHAPTER 4   WRITING TECHNICAL DOCUMENTS IN HTML

Guess the Number

How to play:

The game starts by describing the basic rules: you need to guess a secret number.

```
Guess a random number from 1 to 100
```

Enter your guess for the secret number and the program will provide a hint:

- `Too low` if your guess is too low
- `Too high` if your guess is too high

Let's say the secret number is 33. You might enter `50` as your first guess. The program will print this:

```
Too high
```

For your next guess, you could try the number `25`, which is halfway between 1 and 50. The program then displays:

```
Too low
```

After several more guesses, you eventually enter `33`, and the program prints:

```
That's right!
```

Program Output As Blocks

You can also use `<samp>` and `<kbd>` in a larger block to represent input and output during an interactive session. For example, the "readme" might include a sample run of the "Guess the Number" game so new users can see how to play it. In this case, surround the block with `<pre>` to keep the output on separate lines, and use `<samp>` to format the interactive session.

In this sample "readme" document, I've embedded a stylesheet with `<style>` that provides bold formatting for user input:

```
<!DOCTYPE html>
<html>
  <head>
    <title>Guess the Number</title>
    <style>
      kbd { font-weight: bold; }
```

```
    </style>
  </head>
  <body>
<h1>Guess the Number</h1>

<h2>Sample game:</h2>

<pre><samp>Guess a random number from 1 to 100</samp>
<samp>Your guess?</samp> <kbd>50</kbd> <samp>Too high</samp>
<samp>Your guess?</samp> <kbd>25</kbd> <samp>Too low</samp>
<samp>Your guess?</samp> <kbd>33</kbd> <samp>Too high</samp>
<samp>Your guess?</samp> <kbd>30</kbd> <samp>That's right!
</samp></pre>
  </body>
</html>
```

Guess the Number

Sample game:

```
Guess a random number from 1 to 100
Your guess? 50
Too high
Your guess? 25
Too low
Your guess? 33
Too high
Your guess? 30
That's right!
```

You can add other HTML elements to provide other formatting. For example, to show how to run the game and play it, you might use a `<span>` around the shell prompt and use a stylesheet to apply special formatting. Let's update the previous example to include the Bash command to run the game, and format the $ prompt in italic text:

CHAPTER 4   WRITING TECHNICAL DOCUMENTS IN HTML

```html
<!DOCTYPE html>
<html>
  <head>
    <title>Guess the Number</title>
    <style>
      samp.shell { text-decoration: underline; }
      samp.prompt { font-style: italic; }
      kbd { font-weight: bold; }
    </style>
  </head>
  <body>
<h1>Guess the Number</h1>

<h2>Sample game:</h2>

<pre><samp class="shell">$</samp> <kbd>bash guess.bash</kbd>
<samp>Guess a random number from 1 to 100</samp>
<samp class="prompt">Your guess?</samp> <kbd>50</kbd>
<samp>Too high</samp>
<samp class="prompt">Your guess?</samp> <kbd>25</kbd>
<samp>Too low</samp>
<samp class="prompt">Your guess?</samp> <kbd>33</kbd>
<samp>Too high</samp>
<samp class="prompt">Your guess?</samp> <kbd>30</kbd>
<samp>That's right!</samp></pre>
  </body>
</html>
```

  The $ prompt is technically output from the computer, so it is fair to include as a `<samp>` block. This example uses `class="shell"` to indicate the $ prompt is from the shell, not the program.

CHAPTER 4   WRITING TECHNICAL DOCUMENTS IN HTML

Guess the Number

Sample game:

```
$ bash guess.bash
Guess a random number from 1 to 100
Your guess? 50
Too high
Your guess? 25
Too low
Your guess? 33
Too high
Your guess? 30
That's right!
```

CHAPTER 5

Try It: Writing Your Own Web Pages

Websites are a great way to share information. While most modern websites are constructed using a web content management system like Drupal or WordPress, knowing how to create a website by writing HTML can be a handy skill.

In one example from my own career, my team needed to share certain statistics from an internal server, to make those numbers available to other teams that we needed to coordinate with. Providing the numbers on demand was impossible for one person; that would essentially become a full-time job. Instead, we created a script that generated a web page to display the statistics. By writing a little HTML, and some automation, we were able to share an almost live view into the statistics.

Elements and Structure

HTML is a simple hypertext markup language that is easy for humans to write and for computers to generate automatically. The core of HTML is the element or the tag. From the earlier chapters in this book, we've seen that the basic structure of a web page contains the `<!DOCTYPE html>` declaration on the first line, followed by a well-defined outline with `<html>` that contains both `<head>` and `<body>` sections.

CHAPTER 5   TRY IT: WRITING YOUR OWN WEB PAGES

```
<!DOCTYPE html>
<html>
  <head>
    <title>..</title>
  </head>
  <body>
  ..
  </body>
</html>
```

This is enough to create a basic web page, such as a document that happens to be written in HTML and displayed on the web. But there's not enough structure in place to make this a full website.

Most web pages follow a general outline: a header and navigation bar at the top, main content in the middle, and a footer at the bottom. There's no requirement to include exactly those sections in a web page, but it's a good starting point.

The HTML version 5 standard provides elements that support this kind of structure. These elements are called semantic elements because the name implies their meaning, such as `<header>` for a header, `<nav>` for site navigation, `<main>` for main content, and `<footer>` for the footer. Let's add to the HTML code sample to include these extra tags:

```
<!DOCTYPE html>
<html>
  <head>
    <title>..</title>
  </head>
  <body>
    <header>
      ..
    </header>
```

```
    <nav>
      ..
    </nav>
    <main>
      ..
    </main>
    <footer>
      ..
    </footer>
  </body>
</html>
```

Your web page content goes inside these blocks. Some of these elements can be repeated in a web page; for example, you could include site navigation in the page header, the main body, and the footer. It doesn't really matter where you place these elements in a web page, although it makes the most sense for a web page to have at least a `<header>`, `<main>`, and `<footer>` section in the top level of the page, as a direct descendant of the `<body>` block. This provides a hint to assistive technologies like screen readers, to let the visitor know that a `<header>` immediately inside `<body>` is a site-wide banner, which usually includes a logo, company name, and important links.

To get started, let's define a simple web page that uses a few common tags:

- `<h1>` for the top-level heading, as the page title
- `<h2>` to add subheadings within the body of the page
- `<p>` for paragraphs
- `<em>` to add emphasis and `<strong>` for strong emphasis

- `<a href="..">` to link to other pages on the website
- `<img src=".." alt="..">` for images, with alternative text

With these new tags, we can expand the sample HTML outline to define a simple but functional web page.

```html
<!DOCTYPE html>
<html lang="en">
  <head>
    <title>Sample website</title>
  </head>
  <body>
    <header>
      <h1><img src="stats.svg" alt="Website logo"> Sample
      website</h1>
    </header>

    <nav>
      <a href="start.html">Start here</a>
    </nav>

    <main>
      <h2>Welcome</h2>
      <p>You can create a website on your own with a
      little HTML.
      <a href="start.html">Let's get started!</a></p>
    </main>

    <footer>
      <p>Websites are a great way to share information with
      others.</p>
```

CHAPTER 5   TRY IT: WRITING YOUR OWN WEB PAGES

```
    </footer>
  </body>
</html>
```

That's not a very detailed website, but it's enough of an example that we can work with it. This sample includes the main parts of a web page: a header, navigation links, main body, and footer. When viewed in a web browser, the page generates a very basic, unstyled website:

Sample website

Start here

Welcome

You can create a website on your own with a little HTML. Let's get started!

Websites are a great way to share information with others.

A plain web page using basic HTML

Change the Look

Most modern websites don't use such a plain design. You can improve the look of this web page by applying a stylesheet. The stylesheet can be loaded as a separate file using `<link rel="stylesheet" href="..">` or the styles can be embedded in the `<head>` section with a `<style>` block. Either solution will allow us to make the web page look the way we want it to. Using a separate file allows every page in the website to use the same look and feel, giving the website a cohesive user experience.

The format of a stylesheet is quite different from HTML. Styles are defined in a stylesheet by typing the name of an element or tag to modify, then listing the different styles that can apply to it. These style definitions go inside curly braces, much like a C program. For example, this basic stylesheet defines the background color and text color for the entire page, by modifying the `body` element:

CHAPTER 5   TRY IT: WRITING YOUR OWN WEB PAGES

```
body {
  background-color: white;
  color: black;
}
```

If you're just learning how to create web pages, I recommend starting with just the basics of stylesheet instructions. For this example, we'll use only a few:

- `background-color` to set the background color
- `color` to define the text color
- `text-align` for left, right, and center alignment
- `margin` to add space outside a block element
- `padding` to add space inside an element

Let's embed a stylesheet in the HTML example, by adding a link relationship to a stylesheet using `<link rel="stylesheet" href="..">` in the `<head>` section. The rest of the HTML remains the same:

```html
<!DOCTYPE html>
<html lang="en">
  <head>
    <title>Sample website</title>
    <link rel="stylesheet" href="grayscale.css">
  </head>
  <body>
    <header>
      <h1><img src="stats.svg" alt="Website logo"> Sample
      website</h1>
    </header>

    <nav>
      <a href="start.html">Start here</a>
```

```
    </nav>

    <main>
      <h2>Welcome</h2>
      <p>You can create a website on your own with a
      little HTML.
      <a href="start.html">Let's get started!</a></p>
    </main>

    <footer>
      <p>Websites are a great way to share information with
      others.</p>
    </footer>
  </body>
</html>
```

The HTML provides the content to the web browser, but the stylesheet tells the browser how the content should appear. Let's examine each of these style definitions:

The body definition sets the page body to have a plain white background, and all text on the page to be printed in black. Because the <body> tag is the parent or root of all other elements in an HTML page, this means that all text in any following elements will also be printed in black, unless they change the text color.

```
body {
  background-color: white;
  color: black;
}
```

The header uses a medium gray background with white text. Because the header is a block element, it will be drawn on the web page as a rectangle. I've also added 20 pixels of space inside the rectangle, so the text will be more readable. This also centers the text in the page header.

```
header {
  background-color: gray;
  color: white;
  padding: 20px;
  text-align: center;
}
```

Headings like <h1> come with some default spacing above and below the text, similar to the spacing above and below a paragraph. This extra spacing can sometimes make the page header look weird if there's not enough room for that space in the header's padding, so I've reset h1 to have zero margin:

```
h1 {
  margin: 0;
}
```

The navigation links use a light gray background color, with 10 pixels of extra padding inside the area so the links don't seem crowded. These links are also centered within the box.

```
nav {
  background-color: lightgray;
  padding: 10px;
  text-align: center;
}
```

By default, web browsers will display links in a bright blue color, switching to dark blue after you've clicked into a link. To make this sample easier to read in print, I've set the default link color to be plain black.

```
a {
  color: black;
}
```

Finally, I've helped the page footer to stand apart from the rest of the content by setting it in a black rectangle, but using bright white for the footer text. This also adds 30 pixels of extra space within the footer box, and centers all text.

```
footer {
  background-color: black;
  color: white;
  padding: 30px;
  text-align: center;
}
```

These style elements maintain a "grayscale" color theme, which makes it easy to print in a book, but includes enough additional styling that the web page no longer looks plain:

The same web page but with a grayscale theme

Update the Styles

With stylesheets, you can completely change the look of a website without having to update the HTML. Let's create a new stylesheet that uses a more interesting color palette and more modern fonts. For this version, we'll use

CHAPTER 5   TRY IT: WRITING YOUR OWN WEB PAGES

white text in a dark red background color for the header, dark blue links in a gold navigation bar, and a dark gray footer with white text. The only change we need to make is to reference a different stylesheet file in the `<head>` section of the document:

```
<!DOCTYPE html>
<html lang="en">
  <head>
    <title>Sample website</title>
    <link rel="stylesheet" href="color.css">
  </head>
  <body>
    <header>
      <h1><img src="stats.svg" alt="Website logo">
      Sample website</h1>
    </header>

    <nav>
      <a href="start.html">Start here</a>
    </nav>

    <main>
      <h2>Welcome</h2>
      <p>You can create a website on your own with a
      little HTML.
      <a href="start.html">Let's get started!</a></p>
    </main>

    <footer>
      <p>Websites are a great way to share information with
      others.</p>
    </footer>
  </body>
</html>
```

Just by loading a new stylesheet, we have dramatically changed the appearance of the web page. The new styles use fonts and other style choices that make the content easier to read, and colors that bring a modern appearance to the web page. For example, the body section specifies the same black on white colors but loads a sans-serif font at 12-point size for the text.

```
body {
  background-color: white;
  color: black;
  font-family: sans-serif;
  font-size: 12pt;
}
```

The `font-family` style loads a specific font name, called a family; popular font families that you may recognize include Arial, Times New Roman, and Verdana. Font names that include spaces, like Times New Roman, must be enclosed in spaces, such as:

```
font-family: "Times New Roman";
```

When loading a specific font, it's important to remember that the person visiting the web page may or may not have that font installed on their system. This used to be a much larger problem until Microsoft released its "core fonts for the web" in 1996, which essentially established a de facto assumption that at least these fonts would be available everywhere. The fonts included Andale Mono, Arial, Comic Sans MS, Courier New, Georgia, Impact, Times New Roman, Trebuchet MS, and Verdana. While these fonts are no longer available for free from Microsoft's website, most operating systems either include the font by default or provide a suitable alternative that can be accessed using the same name.

However, not all systems support these fonts. As a fallback, you should always provide several alternative font choices in the `font-family` style. For example, instead of specifying just Times New Roman, the `font-family` line might also list Georgia as an alternative; if Times New Roman is not available for the browser attempting to display the web page, the browser will instead try to load Georgia.

The list of alternative fonts can be quite long, if needed, but most websites specify a preferred font with an alternate font, then list a generic font family for the last fallback. Every web browser supports at least three fonts: `serif`, `sans-serif`, and `monospace`. HTML actually supports other generic font names, but these three font families should cover typical use cases for writing documentation on the web.

The updated stylesheet also specifies a maroon header, gold navigation bar, and dim gray footer. The `<h1>` heading is set to 25 pixels; font sizes are usually specified in either points with `pt` or pixels with `px`. Other styles are updated, but otherwise not too different from the grayscale version:

```
body {
  background-color: white;
  color: black;
  font-family: sans-serif;
  font-size: 12pt;
}
header {
  background-color: maroon;
  color: white;
  padding: 50px;
  text-align: center;
}
h1 {
  font-size: 25px;
  margin: 0;
```

```
}
nav {
  background-color: gold;
  padding: 15px;
  text-align: center;
}
a {
  color: midnightblue;
}
main {
  margin: 100px;
}
footer {
  background-color: dimgray;
  color: white;
  padding: 75px;
  text-align: center;
}
```

    The result is a website that grabs attention, yet remains readable. The extra space inside the header and footer is typical of many websites, and the much larger 100-pixel margin for the main section helps to "offset" the body text from the rest of the web page content.

CHAPTER 5   TRY IT: WRITING YOUR OWN WEB PAGES

The same web page with a color theme

CHAPTER 6

Write Dynamic Web Documentation with JavaScript

Documentation might need to reach a wide audience. A single "readme" file that describes how to use the software may need to be approachable for both experts and newbies. Experts probably don't need as many hints; new users will need more help for a gentler "on ramp" to use the system.

Writing documentation that will be equally useful to both groups is a challenging task. This requires writing descriptions that strike a balance between "detailed technical information" and "providing an overview." This is a difficult writing task, even for very experienced technical writers.

For cases where you need to write one document that supports a wide range of experienced or inexperienced users, consider writing dynamic documentation.

Structuring Content with Classes

One way to create dynamic documentation is with JavaScript. The JavaScript language is a very loose programming language that runs inside web browsers and can modify the HTML document while the user views it.

CHAPTER 6   WRITE DYNAMIC WEB DOCUMENTATION WITH JAVASCRIPT

One example of using JavaScript in a web page is to "attach" an action to a button that a user can click to hide or display certain content. This simple action to toggle between a "hidden" and "visible" state can be a powerful tool in writing documentation on the web.

Let's start with an example for a simple "guess the number" game: the computer generates a secret number in the range from 1 to 100, and the user must find the number by making guesses. After each guess, the computer provides a hint: "too low" or "too high."

A less experienced user might make naive guesses to "walk" their way up to the answer: 10, 20, 30, and so on. This guessing method is quite slow; if the hint for 10 is "too low," that means the secret value is between 11 and 100.

Most experienced users know to apply a binary search algorithm, where you split the possible range of answers in half. For example, a first guess of 50 reduces the possible answers in half; a hint of "too high" means the number is between 1 and 49; a hint of "too low" means the secret value is between 51 and 100. The next guess might be 25, which again reduces the solution in half, and so on for further guesses.

We can include all of these extra details in a single document, and make it approachable for both experts and newbies alike; only the new users will need to see the notes about how to improve their next guess.

The key to this is to include the extra information in a structure within the HTML that JavaScript can either expose or hide at the click of a button. So far, we've learned that HTML has elements that are written as tags. For example, we define a top-level heading in a document with the `h1` element, by writing the `<h1>` tag. But there's more to writing HTML than just elements.

Elements may also have attributes, which are added to the tag. We've seen a few of these already; for example, links use the `a` element, using the `href` attribute for the hypertext reference. A link tag like `<a href="about.html">` is actually three parts:

CHAPTER 6   WRITE DYNAMIC WEB DOCUMENTATION WITH JAVASCRIPT

1. The element is a
2. The attribute is href
3. The attribute value is about.html

In the case of the <a> tag, the href attribute is required. Not all HTML elements require an attribute, although all elements can accept an attribute if one is provided. A typical attribute you might use is class, which you can then use to selectively apply styles within the document.

Let's explore this with a new example, then we can come back to the topic of writing for two audiences. Consider this simple HTML document with just two paragraphs: each paragraph has a class attribute, but different attribute values. This allows a stylesheet in the document to apply a different style to each paragraph, even though both use the <p> tag:

```
<!DOCTYPE html>
<html>
  <head>
    <title>Reminders about audience</title>
  </head>
  <body>

  <p class="intro">It's important to remember that there can be many possible audiences for a document.</p>

  <p class="note">Not every person who reads your document will be an expert. New users may need extra information to get started.</p>

  </body>
</html>
```

53

CHAPTER 6   WRITE DYNAMIC WEB DOCUMENTATION WITH JAVASCRIPT

We can add a stylesheet to format each paragraph in a different way, even though they both use the `<p>` tag. Using a dot in the stylesheet allows us to specify the class that's used by an element on the page. For example, we might format any paragraph with the `intro` class to use bold for the font weight, and any paragraph with the `note` class to use italic as the font style.

```
<!DOCTYPE html>
<html>
  <head>
    <title>Reminders about audience</title>
    <style>
      p.intro { font-weight: bold; }
      p.note { font-style: italic; }
    </style>
  </head>
  <body>

<p class="intro">It's important to remember that there can be many possible audiences for a document.</p>

<p class="note">Not every person who reads your document will be an expert. New users may need extra information to get started.</p>

  </body>
</html>
```

When viewed in a web browser, the first paragraph shows up in bold because that is the paragraph with `class="intro"`. The second paragraph uses `class="note"` so it is printed in italic text:

It's important to remember that there can be many possible audiences for a document.

Not every person who reads your document will be an expert. New users may need extra information to get started.

Using classes to style paragraphs

CHAPTER 6   WRITE DYNAMIC WEB DOCUMENTATION WITH JAVASCRIPT

Use Classes for Each Audience

Let's return to the goal of writing one document that will be readable for both experts and nonexperts. The key to selectively styling text is to set the `class` attribute. You can use any kind of value for this attribute; it's usually best to use a meaningful name like `expert` for text meant for an expert audience and `hint` for hints that will aid a nonexpert reader.

In Chapter 4, we created a "readme" document about the "guess the number" game. That example focused on using `<samp>` to indicate sample output and `<kbd>` for user input. Let's use this as a starting point to add hints about how to play the game using a binary search pattern:

```
<!DOCTYPE html>
<html>
  <head>
    <title>Guess the Number</title>
  </head>
  <body>
<h1>Guess the Number</h1>

<h2>How to play:</h2>

<p>The game starts by describing the basic rules: you need
to guess a secret number.</p>

<pre><samp>Guess a random number from 1 to 100</samp></pre>

<p>Enter your guess for the secret number and the program
will provide a hint:</p>

<ul>
  <li><samp>Too low</samp> if your guess is too low</li>
  <li><samp>Too high</samp> if your guess is too high</li>
</ul>
```

55

```
<p>Let's say the secret number is 33. You might enter
<kbd>50</kbd> as your first guess. The program will print this:</p>

<pre><samp>Too high</samp></pre>

<p>For your next guess, you could try the number <kbd>25</kbd>,
which is halfway between 1 and 50. The program then displays:</p>

<pre><samp>Too low</samp></pre>

<p>After several more guesses, you eventually enter <kbd>33</kbd>,
and the program prints:</p>

<pre><samp>That's right!</samp></pre>
  </body>
</html>
```

Now let's add some extra text to provide a hint about how to find the secret number more quickly. Add a paragraph before the first guess, with class="hint" as its attribute value:

```
<p class="hint">A good approach to guess the number more
quickly is to divide the possible searches by half. For each
guess, pick a number that's in the middle of the range.</p>
```

At the same time, let's add a stylesheet that formats our hint in italic text. This allows the hint to stand apart from the rest of the text, and gives us a starting point to add new styles later:

```
<!DOCTYPE html>
<html>
  <head>
    <title>Guess the Number</title>
    <style>
      p.hint { font-style: italic; }
    </style>
```

CHAPTER 6   WRITE DYNAMIC WEB DOCUMENTATION WITH JAVASCRIPT

```
  </head>
  <body>
<h1>Guess the Number</h1>

<h2>How to play:</h2>

<p>The game starts by describing the basic rules: you need
to guess a secret number.</p>

<pre><samp>Guess a random number from 1 to 100</samp></pre>

<p>Enter your guess for the secret number and the program
will provide a hint:</p>

<ul>
  <li><samp>Too low</samp> if your guess is too low</li>
  <li><samp>Too high</samp> if your guess is too high</li>
</ul>

<p class="hint">A good approach to guess the number more
quickly is to divide the possible searches by half. For each
guess, pick a number that's in the middle of the range.</p>

<p>Let's say the secret number is 33. You might enter <kbd>50</kbd>
as your first guess. The program will print this:</p>

<pre><samp>Too high</samp></pre>

<p>For your next guess, you could try the number
<kbd>25</kbd>, which is halfway between 1 and 50. The program
then displays:</p>

<pre><samp>Too low</samp></pre>

<p>After several more guesses, you eventually enter <kbd>33</kbd>,
and the program prints:</p>
```

57

```
<pre><samp>That's right!</samp></pre>
  </body>
</html>
```

When we view the new "readme" file in a web browser, we'll see the hint as italic text.

Guess the Number

How to play:

The game starts by describing the basic rules: you need to guess a secret number.

Guess a random number from 1 to 100

Enter your guess for the secret number and the program will provide a hint:

- Too low if your guess is too low
- Too high if your guess is too high

A good approach to guess the number more quickly is to divide the possible searches by half. For each guess, pick a number that's in the middle of the range.

Let's say the secret number is 33. You might enter 50 as your first guess. The program will print this:

Too high

For your next guess, you could try the number 25, which is halfway between 1 and 50. The program then displays:

Too low

After several more guesses, you eventually enter 33, and the program prints:

That's right!

The "readme" file with a hint

Add JavaScript to Control the View

With this `class="hint"` attribute and the `p.hint` style to format it, we have the basic building blocks to format a single document that will be useful to a variety of readers.

We can take things to the next level by adding some extra code to the HTML document that will hide or reveal text depending on what level of information the reader needs to see. For example, let's say we want the default for this document not to show hints to the reader. One way to do

CHAPTER 6   WRITE DYNAMIC WEB DOCUMENTATION WITH JAVASCRIPT

this is to update the stylesheet with `display: none` on the hint, so the browser will not display it:

```
<style>
  p.hint {
    font-style: italic;
    display: none;
  }
</style>
```

However, this will always hide the hint, for everyone, whether or not the reader wants to read it. With a little JavaScript, we can modify the document in real time to toggle the `display` style to either `none` to hide it, or `block` to display it. JavaScript is a handy way to modify web pages, because the JavaScript code can directly interact with the Document Object Model (or DOM) of the web page, and change values like the style information.

For example, this function gets a list of all elements with a `hint` as the class name, then changes each element to set the `display` style to `block`, which ensures the element is displayed on the screen:

```
<script>
function showhints() {
  var list, item;

  list = document.getElementsByClassName("hint");

  for (item = 0; item < list.length; item++) {
    list[item].style.display = "block";
  }
}
</script>
```

59

CHAPTER 6   WRITE DYNAMIC WEB DOCUMENTATION WITH JAVASCRIPT

If we add a button on the web page, and tell the browser to run the showhints function whenever someone clicks the button, the reader can reveal all hints if they need them:

```
<!DOCTYPE html>
<html>
  <head>
    <title>Guess the Number</title>
    <style>
      p.hint {
        font-style: italic;
        display: none;
      }
    </style>
  </head>
  <body>
<h1>Guess the Number</h1>

<h2>How to play:</h2>

<p>The game starts by describing the basic rules: you need
to guess a secret number.</p>

<pre><samp>Guess a random number from 1 to 100</samp></pre>

<p>Enter your guess for the secret number and the program
will provide a hint:</p>

<ul>
  <li><samp>Too low</samp> if your guess is too low</li>
  <li><samp>Too high</samp> if your guess is too high</li>
</ul>
```

```
<p class="hint">A good approach to guess the number more
quickly is to divide the possible searches by half. For each
guess, pick a number that's in the middle of the range.</p>

<p>Let's say the secret number is 33. You might enter <kbd>50</
kbd> as your first guess. The program will print this:</p>

<pre><samp>Too high</samp></pre>

<p>For your next guess, you could try the number <kbd>25</kbd>,
which is halfway between 1 and 50. The program then
displays:</p>

<pre><samp>Too low</samp></pre>

<p>After several more guesses, you eventually enter <kbd>33</
kbd>, and the program prints:</p>

<pre><samp>That's right!</samp></pre>

<div><button onclick="showhints()">Show hints</button></div>
<script>
function showhints() {
  var list, item;

  list = document.getElementsByClassName("hint");

  for (item = 0; item < list.length; item++) {
    list[item].style.display = "block";
  }
}
</script>
  </body>
</html>
```

CHAPTER 6   WRITE DYNAMIC WEB DOCUMENTATION WITH JAVASCRIPT

When viewed in a web browser, the user will be able to click a button to reveal the hints:

Guess the Number

How to play:

The game starts by describing the basic rules: you need to guess a secret number.

Guess a random number from 1 to 100

Enter your guess for the secret number and the program will provide a hint:

- Too low if your guess is too low
- Too high if your guess is too high

Let's say the secret number is 33. You might enter 50 as your first guess. The program will print this:

Too high

For your next guess, you could try the number 25, which is halfway between 1 and 50. The program then displays:

Too low

After several more guesses, you eventually enter 33, and the program prints:

That's right!

[Show hints]

The "readme" file with a button to show hints

Make the JavaScript Flexible for the User

One limitation with this method is that we can only show the hints; once revealed, they cannot be hidden again. For that, we can add another button.

Instead of writing a copy of the `showhints` function that will hide the hints, we can extend the JavaScript function to make it more flexible. Let's add a parameter to the function that sets the `display` style to either `block` or `none`. We should also rename this slightly updated function to something like `togglehints` to reflect that we will either hide or display the hints:

CHAPTER 6   WRITE DYNAMIC WEB DOCUMENTATION WITH JAVASCRIPT

```
<script>
function togglehints(view) {
  var list, item;

  list = document.getElementsByClassName("hint");

  for (item = 0; item < list.length; item++) {
    list[item].style.display = view;
  }
}
</script>
```

When we update the HTML page with this new function, we also need to edit the button to call the `togglehints` function with either `block` to reveal the hints or `none` to hide the hints. The easiest way to do this is by defining two buttons: one to hide hints, and one to show them.

```
<!DOCTYPE html>
<html>
  <head>
    <title>Guess the Number</title>
    <style>
      p.hint {
        font-style: italic;
        display: none;
      }
    </style>
  </head>
  <body>
<h1>Guess the Number</h1>

<h2>How to play:</h2>
```

CHAPTER 6   WRITE DYNAMIC WEB DOCUMENTATION WITH JAVASCRIPT

```
<p>The game starts by describing the basic rules: you need
to guess a secret number.</p>

<pre><samp>Guess a random number from 1 to 100</samp></pre>

<p>Enter your guess for the secret number and the program
will provide a hint:</p>

<ul>
  <li><samp>Too low</samp> if your guess is too low</li>
  <li><samp>Too high</samp> if your guess is too high</li>
</ul>

<p class="hint">A good approach to guess the number more
quickly is to divide the possible searches by half. For each
guess, pick a number that's in the middle of the range.</p>

<p>Let's say the secret number is 33. You might enter <kbd>50</kbd> as your first guess. The program will print this:</p>

<pre><samp>Too high</samp></pre>

<p>For your next guess, you could try the number <kbd>25</kbd>,
which is halfway between 1 and 50. The program then
displays:</p>

<pre><samp>Too low</samp></pre>

<p>After several more guesses, you eventually enter <kbd>33</kbd>,
and the program prints:</p>

<pre><samp>That's right!</samp></pre>

<div>
<button onclick="togglehints('block')">Show hints</button>
<button onclick="togglehints('none')">Hide hints</button>
</div>
```

```
<script>
function togglehints(view) {
  var list, item;

  list = document.getElementsByClassName("hint");

  for (item = 0; item < list.length; item++) {
    list[item].style.display = view;
  }
}
</script>
  </body>
</html>
```

By default, the "readme" document doesn't show any hints.

Guess the Number

How to play:

The game starts by describing the basic rules: you need to guess a secret number.

Guess a random number from 1 to 100

Enter your guess for the secret number and the program will provide a hint:

- Too low if your guess is too low
- Too high if your guess is too high

Let's say the secret number is 33. You might enter 50 as your first guess. The program will print this:

Too high

For your next guess, you could try the number 25, which is halfway between 1 and 50. The program then displays:

Too low

After several more guesses, you eventually enter 33, and the program prints:

That's right!

[Show hints] [Hide hints]

The "readme" file with two buttons to show and hide hints

Clicking either button will show just the text that the user wants to read; to reveal these hints, just click the "Show hints" button and the hint will appear in italic text.

CHAPTER 6   WRITE DYNAMIC WEB DOCUMENTATION WITH JAVASCRIPT

Guess the Number

How to play:

The game starts by describing the basic rules: you need to guess a secret number.

`Guess a random number from 1 to 100`

Enter your guess for the secret number and the program will provide a hint:

- `Too low` if your guess is too low
- `Too high` if your guess is too high

A good approach to guess the number more quickly is to divide the possible searches by half. For each guess, pick a number that's in the middle of the range.

Let's say the secret number is 33. You might enter 50 as your first guess. The program will print this:

`Too high`

For your next guess, you could try the number 25, which is halfway between 1 and 50. The program then displays:

`Too low`

After several more guesses, you eventually enter 33, and the program prints:

`That's right!`

[Show hints] [Hide hints]

Reveal the hints at the click of a button

To remove the hints again, click the "Hide hints" button.

Guess the Number

How to play:

The game starts by describing the basic rules: you need to guess a secret number.

`Guess a random number from 1 to 100`

Enter your guess for the secret number and the program will provide a hint:

- `Too low` if your guess is too low
- `Too high` if your guess is too high

Let's say the secret number is 33. You might enter 50 as your first guess. The program will print this:

`Too high`

For your next guess, you could try the number 25, which is halfway between 1 and 50. The program then displays:

`Too low`

After several more guesses, you eventually enter 33, and the program prints:

`That's right!`

[Show hints] [Hide hints]

CHAPTER 6   WRITE DYNAMIC WEB DOCUMENTATION WITH JAVASCRIPT

Remove the hints by clicking the "hide" button

If your project requires you write multiple documents that support audiences at different levels, consider using this method to publish once and read twice. Writing a single document is easier to maintain in a project, and using a few lines of JavaScript to let the user control the view makes it easier to share the document so everyone can use it.

CHAPTER 7

Introduction to Markdown

Markdown was created in the mid-2000s as a way to make it easier to write documentation without having to know markup systems like HTML. At the time, many developers wrote documentation such as "readme" files, "how to compile" guides, and other information using plain text. But plain text doesn't carry any syntactic meaning; it's just text.

Meanwhile, HTML provides a rich set of tags to write documentation, including section headings, paragraphs, sample code, emphasis like italic and bold text, links, and other special formatting. But not every developer wanted to learn HTML just to write documentation.

Markdown was meant as a "middle ground" between plain text and markup systems.

Getting Started in Markdown

Markdown documents are just plain text files that use a formatting syntax that most developers were using anyway in plain text files. For example, paragraphs are just lines of text. Start a new paragraph by adding a blank line, then writing more text. Markdown files should be just as easy for humans to read as they are for computers to interpret.

CHAPTER 7   INTRODUCTION TO MARKDOWN

Here's a sample Markdown file to get started:

```
This is a Markdown file. A Markdown file just looks like
regular text. You don't have to worry about where your
lines end, just hit Enter to start a new line.

To turn Markdown into HTML, you either need to run a command
like pandoc, or publish your Markdown file on a website that
displays it as HTML for you.
```

One way to transform a Markdown file is with the `Markdown.pl` script from John Gruber's daringfireball website. Gruber created the original Markdown system in 2004, and the `Markdown.pl` perl script does all the work to convert Markdown files into basic HTML.

I prefer the `pandoc` command, which transforms not just Markdown to HTML, but a long list of other formats into other formats. The `pandoc` program supports a variety of options, but we can get by with only the basics.

Save this file as a new file called `readme.md`, then run `pandoc` to convert from Markdown to HTML. With only the `--from` and `--to` options, pandoc will print the HTML output back to you:

```
$ pandoc --from markdown --to html readme.md
<p>This is a Markdown file. A Markdown file just looks like
regular text. You don't have to worry about where your lines
end, just hit Enter to start a new line.</p>
<p>To turn Markdown into HTML, you either need to run a command
like pandoc, or publish your Markdown file on a website that
displays it as HTML for you.</p>
```

If you prefer to save the output directly to a file, add the `-o` option to indicate an output filename. You can also use the `>` command line redirector to save the output in a file. But for my demonstrations, I'll let pandoc print the output so we can see the transformation in action.

Basic Formatting

Adding text formatting like bold and italic borrows from plain text file conventions. For example, when writing "readme" files in plain text, many developers adopted a common style where italic text was represented with a single underline, such as `_emphasis_` to provide italic text. To suggest bold type, developers either used all capital letters or they used asterisks around the text, using `**strong emphasis**` to provide bold text.

Markdown uses these syntax conventions, although it also allows two underlines to indicate bold text and one asterisk to provide italic text. That means `_italic_` and `*italic*` are the same italic text, as are `**bold**` and `__bold__` are the same bold text. Use the style that best fits your writing style. Personally, I find it easier to use asterisks for everything: `*italic*` and `**bold**`.

As long as the start and ending markers are not too far apart, Markdown will recognize them to create bold and italic text, even if they are inside a word. This allows for some interesting formatting options, such as bold initial letters to explain an acronym. Here's a sample file with both bold and italic text to demonstrate some typical (and not so typical) text formatting with Markdown:

```
**Hi there!** You can use *italic* or **bold** text in Markdown
by using one or two asterisks. You can also use _italic_ or __
bold__ text with one or two underlines.

A typical way to write a document is to use italic text for
*special terms* and for *emphasis*. I prefer to avoid using
**bold** text in the middle of a paragraph, unless I'm
defining an acronym:

PCMCIA stands for **P**eople **C**an't **M**emorize
**C**omputer **I**ndustry **A**cronyms.
```

Let's save that to a file called text.md and process it using the pandoc program. This lets us see the bold and italic text in the finished document:

```
$ pandoc --from markdown --to html text.md
<p><strong>Hi there!</strong> You can use <em>italic</em> or
<strong>bold</strong> text in Markdown by using one or two
asterisks.
You can also use <em>italic</em> or <strong>bold</strong> text
with one or two underlines.</p>
<p>A typical way to write a document is to use italic text for
<em>special terms</em> and for <em>emphasis</em>. I prefer
to avoid using <strong>bold</strong> text in the middle of a
paragraph, unless I'm defining an acronym:</p>
<p>PCMCIA stands for <strong>P</strong>eople
<strong>C</strong>an't
<strong>M</strong>emorize <strong>C</strong>omputer
<strong>I</strong>ndustry <strong>A</strong>cronyms.</p>
```

Add Structure with Headings

Most people find it easier to read a long document if they break up the long text with section headings. Markdown supports headings and subheadings in two ways: one method that I think looks great even before it's been processed by Markdown, and another method that I find easier to type but less nice to read on its own.

To understand how to write headings, it's important to remember that Markdown borrows much of its syntax and style from how people would write documentation in plain text. To indicate a top-level heading, such as the document's title, authors might have typed the name in all capital letters.

However, uppercase text can be difficult to read, so some authors adopted a slightly different style: underlined the title with a row of equal signs. When typed in a file, this looks a bit like a double underline, suggesting an important title:

```
Readme
======
 
Start here for a quick start guide for how to use the program.
```

Notice that this sample also included a blank line after the row of equal signs and before the first paragraph. This provides a bit of separation from the title and the rest of the text.

To add subheadings to the document, such as usage information, detailed description, and explanation of the options, many authors used a slightly different "underline" style using a row of dashes. This suggests a single underline, to imply a subheading:

```
Readme
======
 
Start here for a quick start guide for how to use the program.

Usage
-----

**readfile** *options*.. *file*..

Description
-----------

The **readfile** program reads one or more data files
into memory.

Options
-------

**-v** Verbose

**-h** Help
```

Let's save this "readme" in a new file called readfile.md, then use the pandoc command to transform it from Markdown into HTML:

```
$ pandoc --from markdown --to html readfile.md
<h1 id="readme">Readme</h1>
<p>Start here for a quick start guide for how to use the
program.</p>
<h2 id="usage">Usage</h2>
<p><strong>readfile</strong> <em>options</em>..
<em>file</em>..</p>
<h2 id="description">Description</h2>
<p>The <strong>readfile</strong> program reads one or more data
files into memory.</p>
<h2 id="options">Options</h2>
<p><strong>-v</strong> Verbose</p>
<p><strong>-h</strong> Help</p>
```

Another way to write section headings is with hash symbols. This looks a bit weird if you display the Markdown document as a plain file, but I find it is easier to type. To write a top-level heading, such as the document's title, type a "hash" # symbol at the start of the line:

```
# Readme

Start here for a quick start guide for how to use the program.
```

Think of each heading and subheadings and "heading levels" and the hash marks make more sense. For example, to add a subheading, or a *second-level* heading, use two hash marks:

```
## Description

The **readfile** program reads one or more data files
into memory.
```

You can add further subheadings, to six different levels, by adding more hash marks. With these heading levels, you can create a more logical structure to your document than you could achieve with the simpler "underline" effect. Let's demonstrate by rewriting the "readme" file to use three heading levels:

```
# Readme

Start here for a quick start guide for how to use the program.

## Description

The **readfile** program reads one or more data files
into memory.

## Usage

**readfile** *options*.. *file*..

### Options

**-v** Verbose

**-h** Help
```

This restructured document moves the program description at the top, and includes the list of options as a new section "under" the usage. If we process the document through pandoc, we can see the generated HTML now includes <h1>, <h2>, and <h3> heading levels:

```
$ pandoc --from markdown --to html readfile2.md
<h1 id="readme">Readme</h1>
<p>Start here for a quick start guide for how to use the
program.</p>
<h2 id="description">Description</h2>
```

```
<p>The <strong>readfile</strong> program reads one or more data
files into memory.</p>
<h2 id="usage">Usage</h2>
<p><strong>readfile</strong> <em>options</em>..
em>file</em>..</p>
<h3 id="options">Options</h3>
<p><strong>-v</strong> Verbose</p>
<p><strong>-h</strong> Help</p>
```

Markdown Makes It Easy

Markdown uses common conventions from writing files in plain text to make it easy to write most documentation without having to remember the markup to get you there. You can use formatting that you might already use in your writing, such as underline for _italic_ or emphasis, and asterisks to format text in **bold** for strong emphasis. Let Markdown do the work so you can stay focused on the content and not on how it will look.

CHAPTER 8

Markup with Markdown

Markdown borrows most of its formatting conventions from writing documents in plain text. In the previous chapter, as part of an introduction to Markdown, we learned how to "underline" text with a row of equal signs to format them as major headings, or with a row of dashes to make subheadings. We also learned basic text formatting like two underscores or two asterisks for **bold** text or one underscore or one asterisk for _italic_ text.

But Markdown can do more than just this basic formatting. You need a variety of formatting to create technical documentation. Let's explore some advanced formatting that you can create in Markdown documents.

Ordered and Unordered Lists

Writing information as lists can be very powerful in technical writing. One common example is in writing project documentation: you might list the requirements and dependencies to build a project, then describe the series of steps to compile everything from source code.

To create lists in Markdown, remember that the system was created so that the formatting instructions looked like normal text. For example, to write an unordered list, also called an *unordered* list, in plain text, you might use a hyphen or asterisk at the start of a line to indicate a "bullet" in a list of bullets. Either is acceptable in Markdown.

Unordered lists do not imply any kind of order. You might use this kind of list to give a list of dependencies.

```
To compile this project, you will need:

- GCC (latest version)
- libncurses
- libsql
```

Another way to write this list is with asterisks instead of dashes.

```
To compile this project, you will need:

* GCC (latest version)
* libncurses
* libsql
```

Some authors like to write unordered lists with a plus mark for the "bullet," like this.

```
To compile this project, you will need:

+ GCC (latest version)
+ libncurses
+ libsql
```

Either way will produce the same kind of list in HTML using the <ul> tag for an *unordered list*. We can use pandoc to convert from Markdown to HTML and see the result:

```
$ pandoc --from markdown --to html list.md
<p>To compile this project, you will need:</p>
<ul>
```

```
<li>GCC (latest version)</li>
<li>libncurses</li>
<li>libsql</li>
</ul>
```

To write an ordered list in Markdown, you write it the same way you would in a plain text file: just add numbers before each list item. The numbers provide a list order, such as a sequence of steps.

```
To build and install the project from source code:

1. Run **./configure**
2. Check that everything works
3. Compile with **make**
4. To install, use **make install**
```

When we process this Markdown file, the numbers in the list are automatically transformed into an ordered list:

```
$ pandoc --from markdown --to html build.md
<p>To build and install the project from source code:</p>
<ol type="1">
<li>Run <strong>./configure</strong></li>
<li>Check that everything works</li>
<li>Compile with <strong>make</strong></li>
<li>To install, use <strong>make install</strong></li>
</ol>
```

Markdown is a very forgiving document markup system, and it tries very hard to be flexible to what you meant to do. One way that Markdown does this is by interpreting the 1. as the start of a numbered list; the rest of the list can use any numbers, or they can all start with 1., it doesn't matter to Markdown.

To build and install the project from source code:

1. Run **./configure**
1. Check that everything works
1. Compile with **make**
1. To install, use **make install**

This flexibility means that you can reorder the list, or remove list items entirely. As long as the first list item starts with 1. Markdown will still process the list correctly. For example, we might remove the second list item, since it doesn't really contribute to the document.

To build and install the project from source code:

1. Run **./configure**
3. Compile with **make**
4. To install, use **make install**

This generates a numbered list because the first list item starts with 1. so Markdown treats it as the first item in an ordered list:

```
$ pandoc --from markdown --to html build.md
<p>To build and install the project from source code:</p>
<ol type="1">
<li>Run <strong>./configure</strong></li>
<li>Compile with <strong>make</strong></li>
<li>To install, use <strong>make install</strong></li>
</ol>
```

Block Quotes

Some technical documents benefit from including long quotes. These block quotes might provide background information, situational context, or an email from a developer.

To format quotes, Markdown borrows from a long-standing email convention. When replying to an email using plain text, email clients usually quote the previous email using > greater than symbols before each line in the message. Markdown does the same:

```
> This is a block quote.
> Block quotes are useful to provide background information
> and to quote emails for reference.
```

You don't have to adjust the lines on the input; the paragraph text will get filled when it is converted from Markdown to something else. For example, we can use pandoc to convert this Markdown sample into HTML:

```
$ pandoc --from markdown --to html quote.md
<blockquote>
<p>This is a block quote. Block quotes are useful to provide background information and to quote emails for reference.</p>
</blockquote>
```

Hyperlinks

Links are one of the few areas in Markdown that doesn't look quite like a plain text file. Instead, you need to write the link in a specific format with square brackets [ ] to indicate the link text and parentheses ( ) to provide the destination URL. Here's an example that links back to Apress:

```
[Apress](https://www.apress.com/) publishes an extensive range of technical books on a variety of subjects.
```

The link can appear anywhere on a line, but I usually try to write my links at the start of a new line so they are easier to read as plain text. When the Markdown is converted into HTML, the <a> tag is written so the URL in parentheses becomes the `href` part of the tag, and the text inside square brackets becomes the link text:

```
<p><a href="https://www.apress.com/">Apress</a> publishes an
extensive range of technical books on a variety of subjects.</p>
```

Tables

Creating tables in Markdown is an exercise in "drawing" a table using plain text characters. Imagine how you might represent a table in plain text: each column should be separated by a vertical line, and the header row should be separated from the table body with a horizontal line. Now "draw" a table in a Markdown file with this general layout, such as this sample:

```
| Installation method | Minimum space | Recommended space |
| ------------------- | ------------- | ----------------- |
| Plain system        | 20 MB         | 30 MB             |
| Full system         | 275 MB        | 450 MB            |
```

That looks like a table, more or less. This readability reflects one of the design goals of Markdown, that the source text should be readable by humans, even before it is processed into something else. And when we process the Markdown table into HTML, we can see how this becomes a table with a header row and table body:

```
$ pandoc --from markdown --to html table.md
<table>
<thead>
<tr class="header">
<th>Installation method</th>
<th>Minimum space</th>
<th>Recommended space</th>
</tr>
```

```
</thead>
<tbody>
<tr class="odd">
<td>Plain system</td>
<td>20 MB</td>
<td>30 MB</td>
</tr>
<tr class="even">
<td>Full system</td>
<td>275 MB</td>
<td>450 MB</td>
</tr>
</tbody>
</table>
```

By default, all table data will be left aligned. If you prefer to center one or more columns, add a colon : to each side of the line of dashes for that column. For example, to center the last two columns in the sample, showing the amount of space needed to complete an installation, update the Markdown table like this:

```
| Installation method | Minimum space | Recommended space |
| ------------------- | :-----------: | :---------------: |
| Plain system        | 20 MB         | 30 MB             |
| Full system         | 275 MB        | 450 MB            |
```

When processed, these two columns will be centered:

```
$ pandoc --from markdown --to html table.md
<table>
<thead>
<tr class="header">
```

CHAPTER 8   MARKUP WITH MARKDOWN

```
<th>Installation method</th>
<th style="text-align: center;">Minimum space</th>
<th style="text-align: center;">Recommended space</th>
</tr>
</thead>
<tbody>
<tr class="odd">
<td>Plain system</td>
<td style="text-align: center;">20 MB</td>
<td style="text-align: center;">30 MB</td>
</tr>
<tr class="even">
<td>Full system</td>
<td style="text-align: center;">275 MB</td>
<td style="text-align: center;">450 MB</td>
</tr>
</tbody>
</table>
```

Think of the colons as "weights" on a balance; with a colon on each "end" of a horizontal line, the line is balanced, and text in that column will be centered. With just one colon, such as at the right side of the line, the line is off balance, and text in the column will be aligned to the right side, such as this version of the table, where the space requirements are right-aligned:

```
| Installation method | Minimum space | Recommended space |
| ------------------- | ------------: | ----------------: |
| Plain system        | 20 MB         | 30 MB             |
| Full system         | 275 MB        | 450 MB            |
```

Aligning these columns on the right can make the numbers easier to read and compare, because the "ones" and "tens" columns will line up:

```
$ pandoc --from markdown --to html table.md
<table>
<thead>
<tr class="header">
<th>Installation method</th>
<th style="text-align: right;">Minimum space</th>
<th style="text-align: right;">Recommended space</th>
</tr>
</thead>
<tbody>
<tr class="odd">
<td>Plain system</td>
<td style="text-align: right;">20 MB</td>
<td style="text-align: right;">30 MB</td>
</tr>
<tr class="even">
<td>Full system</td>
<td style="text-align: right;">275 MB</td>
<td style="text-align: right;">450 MB</td>
</tr>
</tbody>
</table>
```

Verbatim Text

Sometimes it's helpful to provide verbatim text in a document. This could be command names, full command lines, sample program output, or variable names. This verbatim text comes in two flavors, inline and block. These mirror the block and inline elements from HTML.

Project documentation might include commands that the user needs to run to compile a project, or a "getting started" documentation might provide sample commands and output to demonstrate how to use the system. These can be inline or block, depending on how you refer to them in a document.

Let's start with inline verbatim text, which might be used in documentation to indicate command names or variables. Earlier, we wrote a few steps as an ordered list for a build document, but the command names were formatted in bold text. This bold formatting helps the commands stand out from the text, but it doesn't imply commands that the user might type. Instead, we might format these commands with verbatim text; change the asterisks to back ticks like this.

```
To build and install the project from source code:

1. Run `./configure`
2. Compile with `make`
3. To install, use `make install`
```

The back ticks indicate the start and end of the inline verbatim text. When translated into HTML, the verbatim text uses the <code> tag to suggest inline code:

```
<p>To build and install the project from source code:</p>
<ol type="1">
<li>Run <code>./configure</code></li>
<li>Compile with <code>make</code></li>
<li>To install, use <code>make install</code></li>
</ol>
```

Use the back ticks whenever you need to format inline verbatim text, such as names of commands, variables, packages, and system libraries. For example, we might also use verbatim text for the package names in an earlier sample showing a list of requirements to build a project, like this:

```
To compile this project, you will need:

* GCC (latest version)
* `libncurses`
* `libsql`
```

Formatting this Markdown as HTML translates the verbatim text as inline code:

```
<p>To compile this project, you will need:</p>
<ul>
<li>GCC (latest version)</li>
<li><code>libncurses</code></li>
<li><code>libsql</code></li>
</ul>
```

Not all verbatim text will be inline. If you need to provide sample program output or include sample source code in a document, you will need to format this text as a block. Markdown supports two methods to format block code samples: a code "fence" with multiple back ticks, or indenting with several spaces before each line.

I find the "fence" method easier to use because I can see the boundaries more easily, so I am less likely to mess up my verbatim text samples. To insert verbatim text as a block, type three back ticks on a new line. Anything that followed this line *until the next line with just three back ticks* will be formatted as verbatim text:

```
This program prints the numbers from 1 to 10:

```

#include <stdio.h>
```
```

CHAPTER 8   MARKUP WITH MARKDOWN

```
int main()
{
  for (int i = 1; i <= 10; i++) {
    printf("%d\n", i);
  }

  return 0;
}
```

If you save this file as code.md and convert it to HTML using pandoc, the lines between the code "fences" will be formatted as block code using <pre> and <code>:

```
$ pandoc --from markdown --to html code.md
<p>This program prints the numbers from 1 to 10:</p>
<pre><code>#include &lt;stdio.h&gt;

int main()
{
  for (int i = 1; i &lt;= 10; i++) {
    printf(&quot;%d\n&quot;, i);
  }

  return 0;
}</code></pre>
```

Another way to format verbatim blocks of text is by inserting four spaces before each line. I'm not fond of this method because my editor doesn't show a mark for spaces, so these are invisible to me; I don't know if I've used four spaces or three. But you may prefer this method, depending on how you like to write documentation.

CHAPTER 8 MARKUP WITH MARKDOWN

Here's the same example with spaces instead of the "fence" method.

This program prints the numbers from 1 to 10:

```
#include <stdio.h>

int main()
{
  for (int i = 1; i <= 10; i++) {
    printf("%d\n", i);
  }

  return 0;
}
```

This sample uses both inline verbatim text with the single back ticks, and block verbatim text using four spaces. This sample could also have used the code "fence" but this shows the "spaces" method to add verbatim text. When this is transformed from Markdown to HTML, the indented text is formatted as a block code sample:

```
$ pandoc --from markdown --to html code.md
<p>This program prints the numbers from 1 to 10:</p>
<pre><code>#include &lt;stdio.h&gt;

int main()
{
  for (int i = 1; i &lt;= 10; i++) {
    printf(&quot;%d\n&quot;, i);
  }

  return 0;
}</code></pre>
```

CHAPTER 8   MARKUP WITH MARKDOWN

One reason I prefer the code "fence" over the "spaces" method for code samples is that the "fence" is easier to use when including code that is sensitive to leading spaces. Python is one example, such as this short program to count from 1 to 10:

```
count = 1

while count <= 10:
    print(count)
    count = count + 1
```

Python uses spaces to indicate when code is a "child" of another block; in this example, the `print(count)` statement and `count = count + 1` iteration are both indented with the same number of spaces, so they are both "children" of the `while` loop. But if the spaces are uneven, the program will not work.

When I write documentation, I prefer the "fence" method because it is less likely to cause problems with spaces and indenting. Consider this Python code sample in a Markdown document, using the "fence" method.

```
This program prints the numbers from 1 to 10:

```
count = 1

while count <= 10:
    print(count)
    count = count + 1
```
```

The code "fence" makes it clear to me, the author, where my code sample begins and ends. It doesn't matter that Python is space sensitive; I can just copy and paste the Python sample code into my Markdown document. As long as the code sample begins and ends with a code "fence," I know the document will be formatted correctly.

Compare this to using the "spaces" method to include the sample Python code. I find the extra spacing quickly becomes distracting.

This program prints the numbers from 1 to 10:

```
count = 1

while count <= 10:
    print(count)
    count = count + 1
```

Inserting this sample Python code into a Markdown file requires adding spaces before each line. Similarly, someone else who copies the code sample from the Markdown file will need to remove the extra spaces before they use it; this is an extra step that is not needed when using the code "fence" method.

CHAPTER 9

GitHub for Technical Writers

Many organizations rely on a source code repository system. Using a source code repository means you can track every change made to a file over time, including details about the update, who made the edit, and their notes about what changed. If it's a plain text file like program source code, or a plain text markup system like Markdown, you can track changes to it in a source code repository.

GitHub and GitLab make it easy to manage and display Markdown documents directly in their system. This method of using the same tools to manage source code as you use to manage documentation is called "Docs as Code." While "Docs as Code" can use any markup file written in plain text, Markdown remains popular on these platforms because many developers already prefer to write documentation in Markdown.

How Source Control Works

Let's look at an example to see what is happening with a source control system. This is a somewhat simple view into source control; GitHub and GitLab are more complex than this model. But this will help explain how things work behind the scenes.

CHAPTER 9   GITHUB FOR TECHNICAL WRITERS

As a technical writer, I might start with a file called readme.md that describes a new project. Once I've created a first draft of this file, I might save it in the source control system. This action is called a *commit* and stores a copy of the file in the source control system as "version 1" or some other tracking number. GitHub and GitLab actually use a different scheme for these "version" labels, but for this demonstration, we'll assume the first commit is "version 1."

readme.md

When we commit the new file, we can also save a comment that describes what changed in the file. This allows us to go back and review the entire edit history of a file by reading the comments.

Source control systems aren't limited to one file at a time; we can also track other files *and entire projects* in the system as well. Let's say I create another file called build.md that describes how to compile the project from source code. After I have a first draft of this file, I commit "version 1" of this file into the source control system.

At the same time, I might update the "readme" file to reference the "build" document; after making this edit, I would commit the new version into the source control system. This call is "version 2" of the readme.md file.

CHAPTER 9   GITHUB FOR TECHNICAL WRITERS

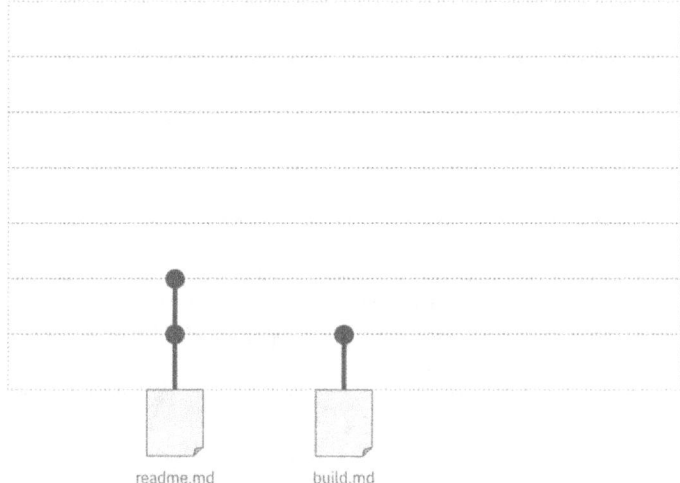

My change to the "readme" file could be quite small, such as fixing a typo, or it could be everything, such as a complete rewrite. If the only change from "version 1" to "version 2" was fixing a typo on one line, the system doesn't need to store the whole "version 2" at once. Instead, the source control system actually saves the *difference* between these two files: only one line changed.

At any time, we can always ask the source control system to give us "version 1" or "version 2" of the `readme.md` file. If we ask for "version 1," the system just gives us a full copy of that file; it was the first version stored, so it has a complete copy. If we ask for "version 2," the system extracts "version 1" of the file, then applies the *differences* to get from "version 1" to "version 2." It's still the same "version 2," but the system did some extra work behind the scenes.

If these two files describe the project, it might be helpful to save a reference to "version 1" of `build.md` and "version 2" of the `readme.md` file. This action is called a *release*, depending on the source control system you're using. When you make a release, the system makes an association between that release label (sometimes called a *tag*) and the versions of each file.

CHAPTER 9   GITHUB FOR TECHNICAL WRITERS

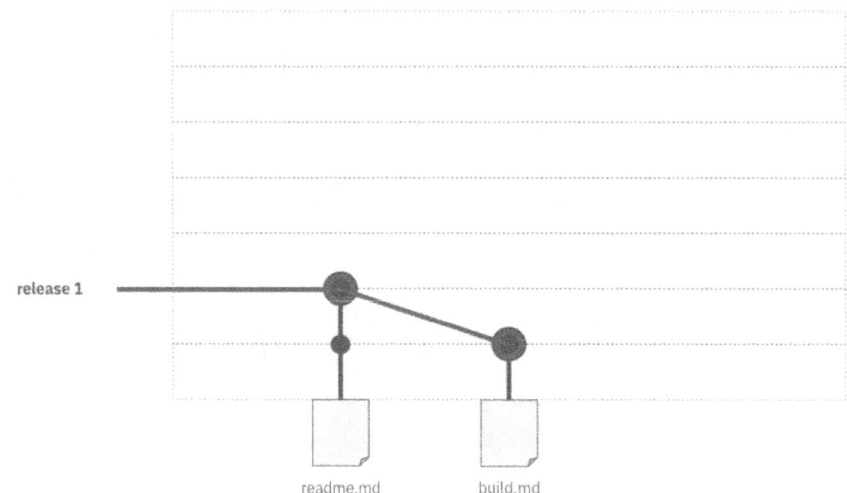

After making this release, we can later ask the source control system for "release 1," and it will generate "version 1" of build.md and "version 2" of the readme.md file.

We can still "unwind" the changes and ask the system to produce an earlier version of any file, or to generate the files and versions associated with "release 1." We can also add other files to the project and continue to edit the files we have. For example, after several more revisions, we might have "version 3" of the readme.md file, "version 2" of build.md, and a new contrib.md that is also at "version 2."

CHAPTER 9   GITHUB FOR TECHNICAL WRITERS

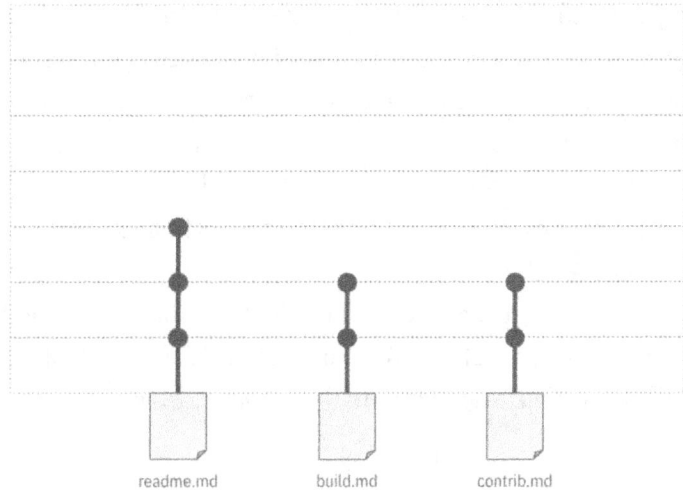

At this point, source code control becomes a way to manage the lifecycle of an entire project. Every commit is tracked, including a comment to describe the change, and we can make releases that bundle up a collection of files at specific versions. For example, we might create a new release called "release 2" for "version 2" of contrib.md, "version 2" of build.md, and "version 3" of the readme.md file, so we can refer back to it later.

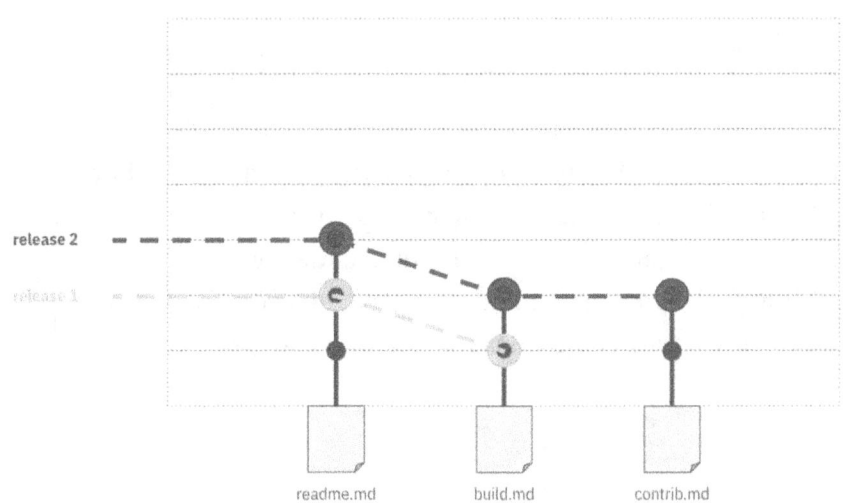

97

Creating a "release 2" tag is just a reference point for all of the files in that release. It doesn't change or overwrite the previous "release 1" associations. Even after adding the contrib.md file, which didn't exist in the earlier release, we can ask the system to generate the "release 1" files and it will only produce "version 2" of readme.md and "version 1" of build.md. It will not generate any version of contrib.md because that file was not included in "release 1."

As time goes on, we might have made further changes to each of these files, and can save "release 3" to associate "version 7" of readme.md, "version 3" of build.md, and "version 5" of contrib.md.

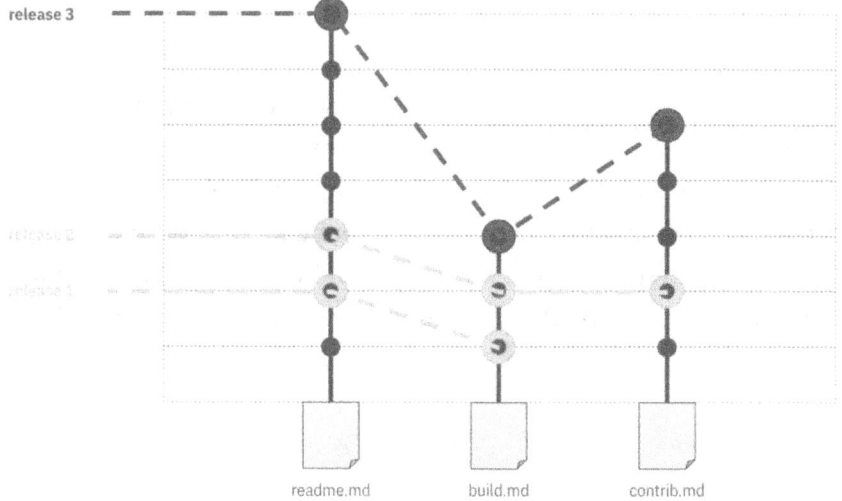

The ability to track versions and releases, including the ability to "roll back the clock" to an earlier version of a file or release of a project, is very useful in project management. The source code control system always tracks what you store in it, which can be useful if you need to compare what changed between two releases of a project or two versions of a file.

CHAPTER 9   GITHUB FOR TECHNICAL WRITERS

Managing Versions in GitHub

Now that we have a good overview of how source code control systems work, let's practice what we've learned by experimenting with a new GitHub project. To follow along, you will need a free GitHub account; sign up at github.com.

Start by clicking the "New" button in GitHub to create a fresh repository:

To demonstrate, I'll create a new generic repository called `project`. GitHub uses the term "repository" to mean a project, so this is a good name to use for this example. For the purposes of this example, it will be safe to use the terms *repository* and *project* interchangeably.

CHAPTER 9   GITHUB FOR TECHNICAL WRITERS

Create a new repository
A repository contains all project files, including the revision history.

Required fields are marked with an asterisk (*).

Owner *   Repository name *

[jhall ▾] / [project]
              ✓ project is available.

Great repository names are short and memorable. Need inspiration? How about reimagined-train ?

Description (optional)

[Sample project]

○ **Public**
   Any logged in user can see this repository. You choose who can commit.

⦿ **Private**
   You choose who can see and commit to this repository.

Initialize this repository with:

☐ **Add a README file**
   This is where you can write a long description for your project. Learn more about READMEs.

Add .gitignore

[.gitignore template: None ▾]

Choose which files not to track from a list of templates. Learn more about ignoring files.

Choose a license

[License: None ▾]

A license tells others what they can and can't do with your code. Learn more about licenses.

ⓘ You are creating a private repository in your personal account.

[**Create repository**]

I do not already have a repository called `project`; GitHub reports that the name `project` is available. GitHub repository names are connected to your GitHub account. Someone else might have another repository called `project` and that's okay; my `project` is not the same as their `project`.

Repositories can be public or local. A public repository will be visible to anyone else who uses GitHub, but a private repository will only be accessible to you. This is a demonstration, not a project I plan to share, so I created this as a private repository.

CHAPTER 9   GITHUB FOR TECHNICAL WRITERS

GitHub also has a few other options to choose from. If I tick the "Add a README" box, GitHub will also create a new README.md file for me. I want to demonstrate how to add files, so I didn't tick that box. The .gitignore option is useful if you use a Git desktop client that can commit files for you; you can use .gitignore to list the names of files and folders that you do *not* want to be tracked by GitHub. Finally, the license menu allows me to choose a license for my project, such as the GNU General Public License or the MIT License for an open source project. This is a demonstration project, so I'll skip this.

After clicking the "Create repository" button, GitHub generates an empty repository for the project. Because there is nothing here yet, GitHub presents a kind of "welcome" screen where I can set up the project. One of these is a blue bar with several links:

Get started by creating a new file or uploading an existing file. We recommend every repository include a README, LICENSE, and .gitignore.

Let's add a new file to the project; click the "creating a new file" link to bring up a web editor where you can name the file and start working on it.

We can enter any kind of source file here; let's test by creating a short Markdown file of a few lines:

101

CHAPTER 9 GITHUB FOR TECHNICAL WRITERS

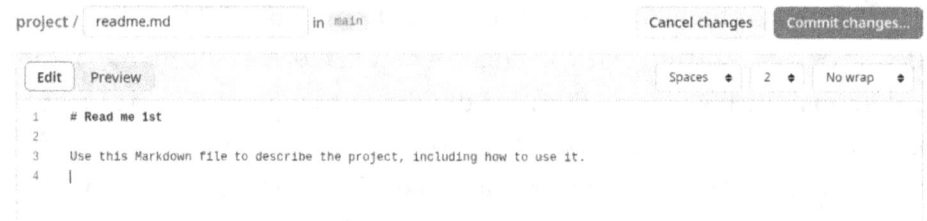

To save "version 1" of this file to GitHub, click the "Commit changes" button in the upper-right corner. Before we commit the new file, GitHub will prompt for a description of the change, so we can track this history later. GitHub suggests a short commit message, which we can update to something more descriptive. The extended description is optional, but is an excellent opportunity to provide a more detailed note about what changed.

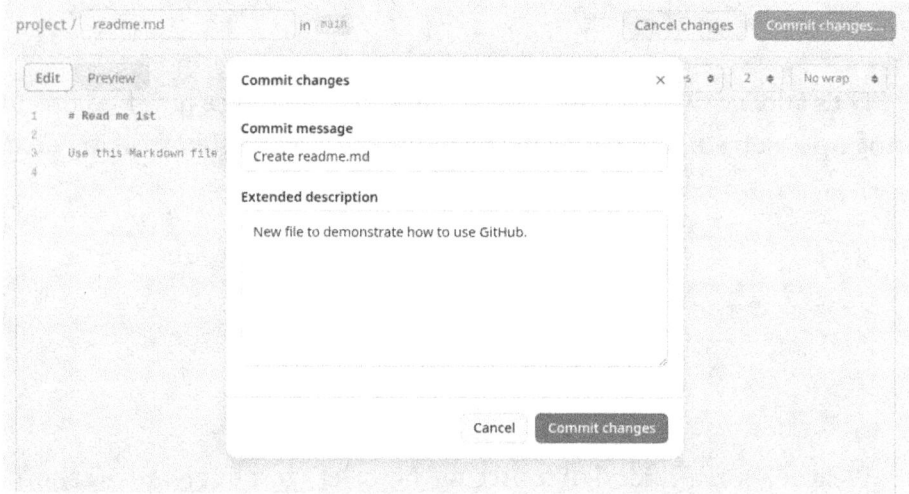

After committing the change, GitHub brings us back to the project's home page, where we can see a "version 1" of our `readme.md` file has been saved to GitHub.

CHAPTER 9 GITHUB FOR TECHNICAL WRITERS

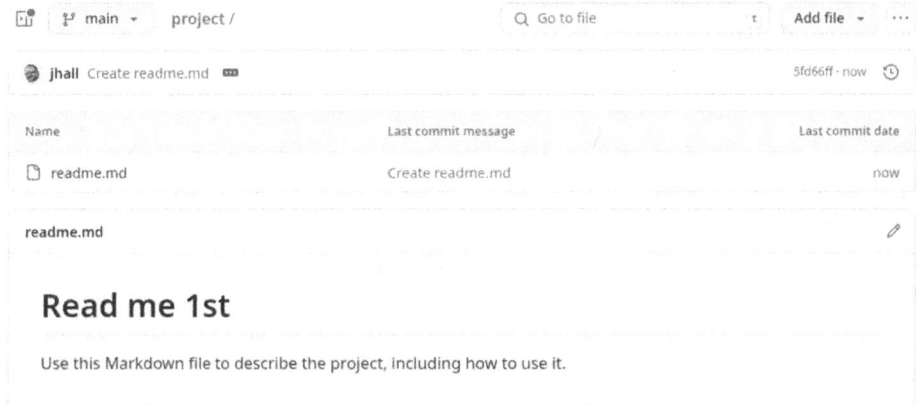

There's lots to explore on this page. The `5fd66ff` message in the upper right, in the box that says "Create readme.md," is actually part of the version label for this file. GitHub doesn't actually label files as "version 1" or "version 2," but instead uses a long string of letters and numbers. This will be unique for every version of every file in GitHub; your number will be different from mine, even if the content is the same.

To see the changes in that commit, click on the version number. You can also see the same change history by clicking the "Create readme.md" text in the file list. This project only has one file in it, so the list is just the `readme.md` file. To view the contents of the file, you can click the name of the file in the file list.

Let's see what changed by clicking on one of the links for the change history:

103

Commit

This shows that the file was last edited about 12 minutes ago, and includes details for the commit: the we added three lines and deleted none. GitHub shows the new lines in green, which is the entire file, because we started with a new file.

Let's modify the document so we can see what other changes like. Click on the filename to view the file, then use the "pencil" icon in the upper right to edit the file:

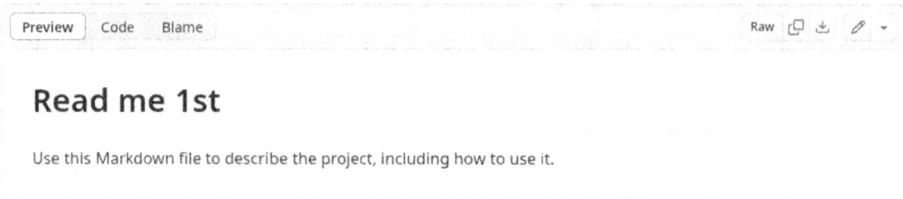

In this case, we'll edit the title from "Read me 1st" to just "Read me." Make the edit, then click the "Commit changes" button to save it:

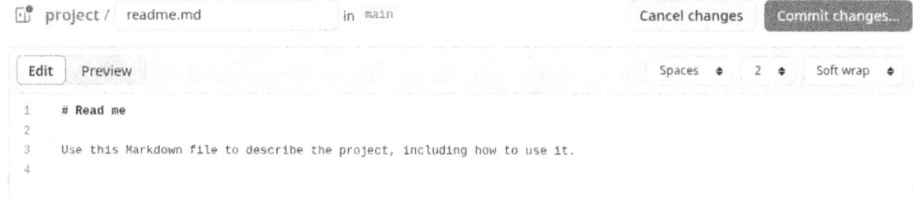

CHAPTER 9 GITHUB FOR TECHNICAL WRITERS

As before, enter the commit message and an extended description for the change. After saving the file, click on the version number in the upper right to view the edit history:

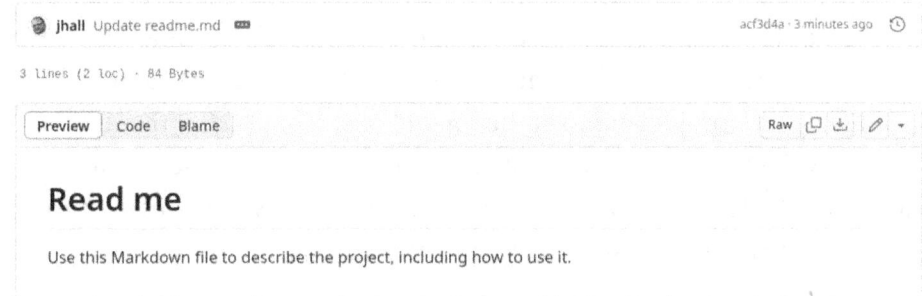

In this example, I changed "Read me 1st" to "Read me," so GitHub shows the old version of the line in red and the new version in green. My specific change (removing "1st") is shown in a slightly darker red:

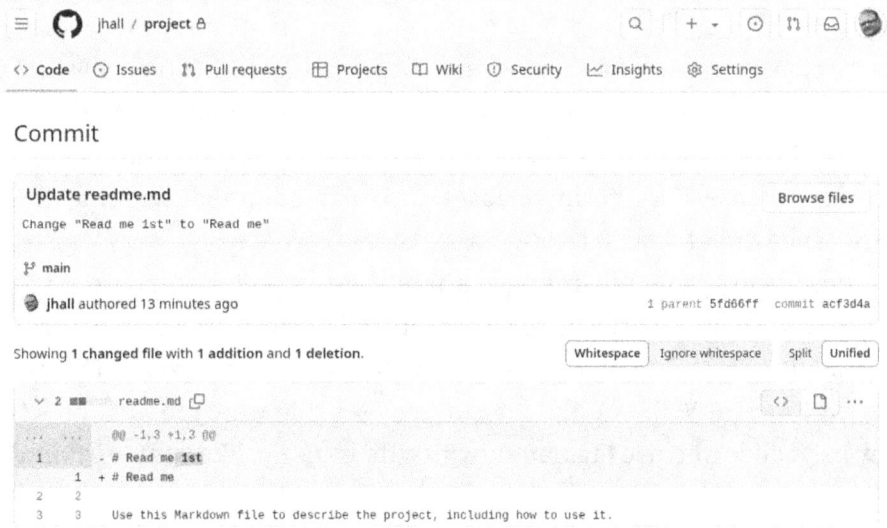

105

This color highlighting represents the *difference* between the first and second versions of the file. If we were to describe this in words, we might say "remove line 1, and add a new line 1." The source control system tracks the same change, using a more compact description that is easier for a computer to automate. But at a high level, GitHub tracks a difference between the two versions that means "remove line 1, and add a new line 1."

Click on the project name at the top of the screen to view the full repository. So far, we've added only one short file to the project, but let's say we're satisfied with what we have. To capture this version of the project, we can create a release using the link on the far right:

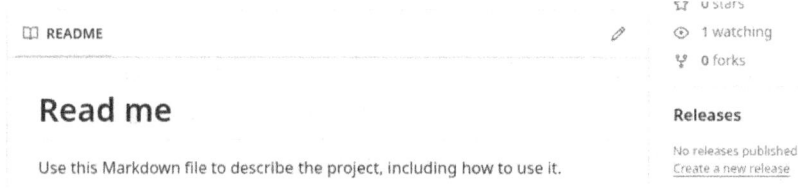

To create a release, we also need to define a *tag*, which typically looks like `release_1` or some similar label. GitHub recommends starting tag names with the letter `v` to indicate a version, plus a number, such as `v1.0.0` for a first release. For interim releases, GitHub recommends adding the word `alpha` or `beta`, such as `v0.9.1_beta`.

Most development teams have established a naming standard for these release tags. For example, early in my career, I worked with a team that used all uppercase tag names with a version number for production-ready releases, such as `VER_1_1`. For interim releases that were meant for testing, they used all lowercase tag names with a date stamp, like `test_20190612`.

CHAPTER 9   GITHUB FOR TECHNICAL WRITERS

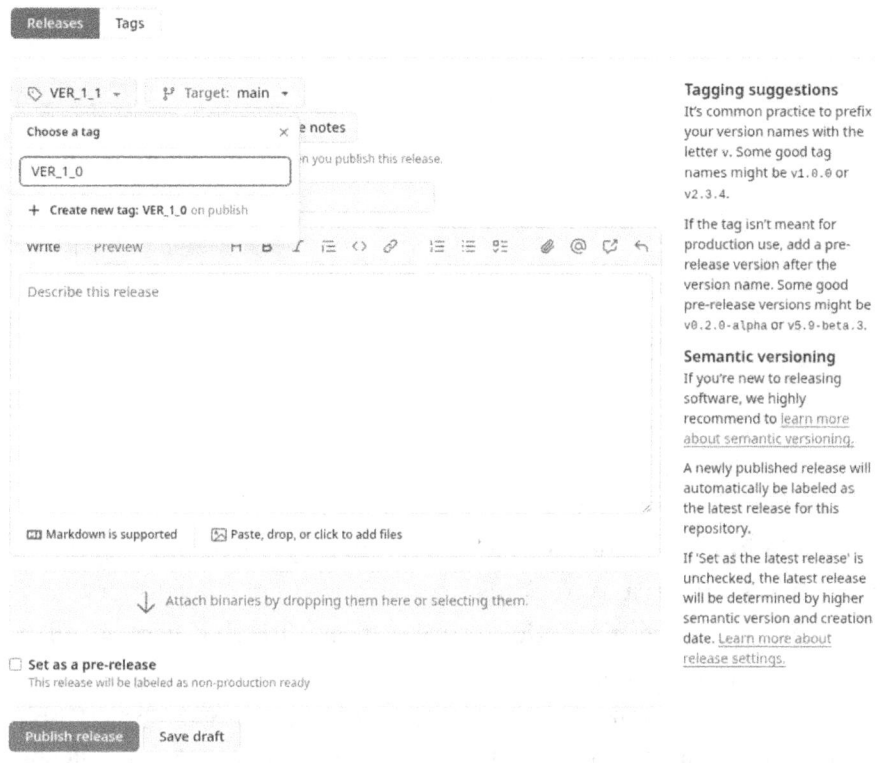

Don't forget to include a release title and describe the release before you click the green "Publish release" button. GitHub will then create an association between this tag name and all versions of all files in the project.

107

CHAPTER 9   GITHUB FOR TECHNICAL WRITERS

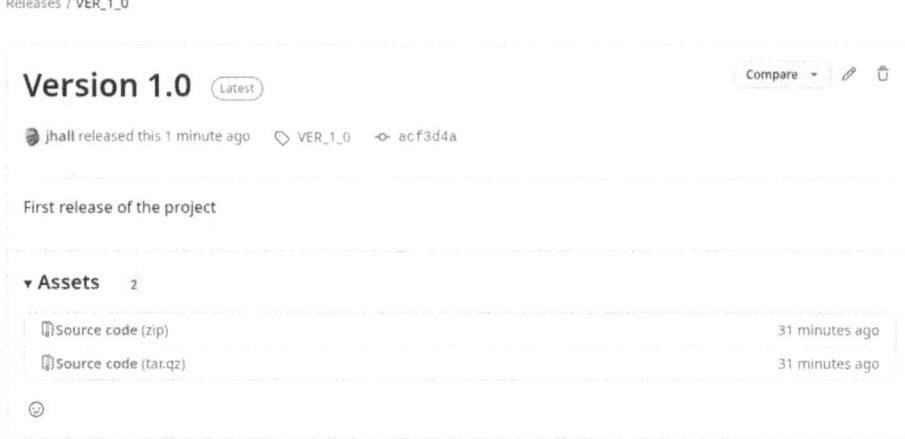

GitHub is a powerful tool to manage projects, including documentation. Like other source code control systems, GitHub lets you manage changes and track history. Because many developers can collaborate using a source code control system, GitHub is very popular with development teams.

Use these tips to get started managing your next project in GitHub. If the project involves other developers, the repository will probably be controlled by another developer, so you should also check with them for their preferences and standards, such as file organization or file names. These tips will help you to quickly get up to speed managing files and revision history with GitHub.

CHAPTER 10

Next Steps

This pocket guide is a focused dive into markup for technical writers. We covered two of the most common markup systems used by technical teams: HTML and Markdown.

HTML is the markup language that drives the World Wide Web. Every web page is written in HTML. It might have JavaScript or something else that provides reactive web pages that respond to you in real time, but at the core, web pages deliver content in HTML format.

That means you can be more effective if you know how to write content in HTML. While you are unlikely to create websites and web pages in HTML entirely by hand, knowing how HTML works "behind the scenes" will help you to create accurate, effective, and accessible content.

Every technical writer I work with uses a web content management system like WordPress, TYPO3, or Drupal to create websites quickly and automate the content creation. But also, every technical writer I work with shares the same story: at some point, something will go wrong in the content system and you'll be left wondering, "Why is my bullet point way over there?" And that's when you need to go into "Source" view to fix it. Now that you know the basics of HTML markup, you can fix broken HTML without breaking other things.

And if you need to, you can create content by hand, too. That's a power skill that can use to create reports, write articles, and generate analysis. You don't need to use a desktop "office" application to write it; you can write the HTML and view the results in a web browser.

CHAPTER 10   NEXT STEPS

Markdown is a minimal markup system that makes it easy to create content quickly and easily, without getting lost in the details. I find that writing in Markdown means I can focus on the content without getting distracted by how it will appear on the screen. That makes me a more efficient technical writer.

But writing with minimal markup doesn't mean giving up powerful formatting. In the last few chapters, we learned that you can format headings and paragraphs, with bold and italic text, which are the basics of technical writing. In addition, you can format code samples, either as inline code or larger blocks of source code, shell scripts, command line output, or other verbatim text. With just a few keystrokes, you can also format links, create ordered and unordered lists, and even generate tables.

Use What You've Learned

Learning how to write with HTML and Markdown also helps you to learn other markup systems later. For example, you can use what we learned about Markdown to learn other minimal-markup systems, such as AsciiDoc. The AsciiDoc system has the same design goals as Markdown, so it looks very similar to Markdown. AsciiDoc files are plain text, paragraphs are lines of text separated by blank lines, and so on.

Specific formatting rules are different between Markdown and AsciiDoc, but these are just a matter of learning the implementation. For example, where Markdown uses either one * or _ to format in italic text, and two ** or __ for bold text, AsciiDoc uses only a single _ for italic and a single * for bold. Headings use equal signs, starting with two == for first-level headings and three === for second-level headings; add more equal signs to indicate further heading levels.

You can apply what you learned from Markdown to this basic understanding of AsciiDoc, and from there, pick up the rest of AsciiDoc in an afternoon. Now that you understand how to write in Markdown, learning a similar system like AsciiDoc is a matter of learning the differences between the two. Even with this basic understanding of AsciiDoc, you can use what you've learned about Markdown to interpret this AsciiDoc file:

```
== Why I love minimal markup

With a minimal markup system like *Markdown* or *AsciiDoc*
I can focus on _what I am writing_ and not get distracted with
_what it will look like_.
```

This is the same as writing this in Markdown:

```
# Why I love minimal markup

With a minimal markup system like **Markdown** or **AsciiDoc**
I can focus on *what I am writing* and not get distracted with
*what it will look like*.
```

Similarly, by learning HTML, you've also "opened the door" to similar tag-based document systems like XML. XML is the e**X**tensible **M**arkup **L**anguage, and it is closely related to HTML. The same "rules" that apply to HTML also apply to XML:

1. XML elements are written as tags
2. Write a tag as a control word between angle brackets
3. Most tags come in pairs: an opening tag and a closing tag

Those are the same rules we learned in Chapter 1 with the basics of HTML. XML follows the same basic rules, but it is more strict in some areas, and more flexible in others. For example, without knowing the specifics of writing in XML-based markup, you can apply what you've learned about HTML to understand what XML markup "means," such as this sample article written in Simplified Docbook:

CHAPTER 10   NEXT STEPS

```
<article>
  <info>
    <title>5 best practices</title>
  </info>

  <section>
    <title>Introduction</title>
    <para>Describe the topic of the report. If you have a
    personal connection to the topic, indicate that here.</para>
  </section>

  <section>
    <title>Recommendations</title>
    <para>Write a few paragraphs to highlight key takeaways,
    then list your recommendations.</para>

    <section>
      <title>Recommendation 1</title>
      <para>Write 2 or 3 paragraphs.</para>
    </section>
    <section>
      <title>Recommendation 2</title>
      <para>Write 2 or 3 paragraphs.</para>
    </section>
    <section>
      <title>Recommendation 3</title>
      <para>Write 2 or 3 paragraphs.</para>
    </section>
    <section>
      <title>Recommendation 4</title>
      <para>Write 2 or 3 paragraphs.</para>
    </section>
    <section>
```

```
      <title>Recommendation 5</title>
      <para>Write 2 or 3 paragraphs.</para>
    </section>
  </section>
</article>
```

Simplified Docbook uses different tags than HTML, and reuses tags for multiple purposes, but you can still leverage what we learned about HTML to interpret the XML markup: Simplified Docbook uses `<info>` for document metadata, such as `<title>` for the article's title, and `<para>` for paragraphs. Sections use `<section>`, which may be nested, each with its own `<title>` for the major or minor headings.

Not every XML-based markup is this naturally descriptive with its tags, but you can carry forward what you know about HTML to learn other XML-based markup. Another example of XML markup is DITA, which borrows some of its formatting tags from HTML. Before you pick up a book that explains how to write with DITA, you can probably understand most of what is in a DITA file, like this sample DITA Concept file:

```
<?xml version="1.0" encoding="UTF-8"?>
<!DOCTYPE concept PUBLIC "-//OASIS//DTD DITA Concept//EN"
"concept.dtd">
<concept id="concept">
  <title>DITA Concept</title>
  <shortdesc>Information about a thing.</shortdesc>
  <conbody>
    <p>Think of DITA Concept like a technical description or
    extended definition: provide information about a thing or
    process. Standard formatting includes
    <b>bold</b>, <i>italic</i>, and <u>underline</u> text.
  </conbody>
</concept>
```

CHAPTER 10   NEXT STEPS

Take It to the Next Level

You don't need a word processor to write documentation for your project. Technical writing can be done with any system, including plain text. But using a markup system like HTML or a minimal markup system like Markdown helps you to write more effective documentation.

GitHub and other source control systems support Markdown by default. Start your next GitHub project by writing a README.md file that describes what the project is about, and other Markdown files to provide an overview of how the code works, how to build the project from source code, and how to use the completed application. With Markdown, you can focus on what you're writing without getting distracted by the formatting to get there.

For fine control over your documentation, use HTML and apply a stylesheet to format it the way you want it to look. With HTML and stylesheets, you have total control over the content and its appearance. Everyone can view what you write; they only need a web browser to access it.

Use this Pocket Guide as a quick reference guide when you write documentation for your next project. With a little practice with HTML and Markdown, you can quickly and easily write professional documentation that anyone can use.

GPSR Compliance

The European Union's (EU) General Product Safety Regulation (GPSR) is a set of rules that requires consumer products to be safe and our obligations to ensure this.

If you have any concerns about our products, you can contact us on

ProductSafety@springernature.com

In case Publisher is established outside the EU, the EU authorized representative is:

Springer Nature Customer Service Center GmbH
Europaplatz 3
69115 Heidelberg, Germany

www.ingramcontent.com/pod-product-compliance
Lightning Source LLC
LaVergne TN
LVHW020413070526
838199LV00054B/3605